a RESOURCE FROM familyLife

preparing for marriage

a complete guide to help you discover god's plan for a lifetime of love

BY DAVID BOEHI, BRENT NELSON, jeff schulte & LLoyd shadrach

DENNIS RAINEY

general editor

Gospel Light

How to Let the Lord Build Your House and not labor in vain.

FamilyLife is a division of Campus Crusade for Christ, Incorporated, an evangelical Christian organization founded in 1951 by Bill Bright. FamilyLife was started in 1976 to help fulfill the Great Commission by strengthening marriages and families and then equipping them to go to the world with the gospel of Jesus Christ. Our FamilyLife Marriage Conference is held in most cities throughout the United States and is one of the fastest-growing marriage conferences in America today. Information on all resources offered by FamilyLife may be obtained by either writing or calling us at the address and telephone number listed below.

GOSPEL LIGHT PUBLISHING STAFF

William T. Greig, Publisher
Dr. Elmer L. Towns, Senior Consulting Publisher
Billie Baptiste, Publisher, Research, Planning and Development
Dr. Gary S. Greig and Wesley Haystead, M.S.Ed., Senior Consulting Editors
Jill Honodel, Editor
Pam Weston, Assistant Editor
Kyle Duncan, Associate Publisher
Bayard Taylor, M.Div., Senior Editor, Theological and Biblical Issues
Debi Thayer, Designer
Steve Bjorkman, Illustrator

Dennis Rainey, Executive Director
FamilyLife
P.O. Box 23840
Little Rock, AR 72221-3840
(501) 223-8663

Published by Gospel Light, Ventura, California 93006
Printed in U.S.A.

contents

INtRODUCtION
BY DeNNIS RaINeY

Not long after I graduated from the University of Arkansas one of
my good friends, a female student at the university, came to me for
counsel. She was dating a young man who happened to be my best
friend, and I knew what was happening in that relationship. She
wanted to marry him, but he was hot and cold, uncertain of whether
he was willing to commit himself to her.

For some reason I had doubts about whether they should marry.
So when she asked me for advice, I told her a parable I had recently
heard.

> A little boy named Johnny was playing marbles in his
> front yard. His uncle drove up and decided to play with
> the boy for a few minutes. Then the uncle reached into
> his pocket and pulled out a dime and a dollar.
>
> "Johnny," he asked, "would you like a dime today or a
> dollar next week?"
>
> Johnny's boyish eyes bounced back and forth between
> the shiny dime and the crisp greenback. He thought, *I
> could buy a bag of potato chips today, or I could wait until
> next week and buy a rubber ball.* He felt some hunger
> pangs, so he grabbed the dime, bought some chips and
> wolfed them down. They were delicious.
>
> A week passed and when Johnny went out to play
> one afternoon he noticed that every other boy in his
> neighborhood had a rubber ball. He wanted one real
> bad, so he rode his bicycle over to his uncle's house.
> "Hey, uncle, how about that dollar you promised me?"
> Johnny asked.
>
> But his uncle looked down and said, "Johnny, last
> week I promised you a dime today or a dollar next week,
> and you made your choice. You can't have the dollar
> now."

When I finished that story, I asked the young lady, "Do you believe that God is big enough to give you someone else later on who you could love more than this guy?"

She thought for a moment and nodded her head yes.

"Perhaps," I said, "God in His sovereignty knows this young man you are dating is a dime and He has a dollar for you later on."

Well, perhaps you've guessed the outcome of my story. That young lady, Barbara Peterson, decided not to marry my best friend. In fact, just over a year later she became my wife. To this day, people find it hard to believe that I really had no mixed motives when we talked that day!

Once in a while Barbara and I pull out our old wedding pictures and gaze in wonder at those youthful faces. There we are posing with our families. There we are reciting our vows. There we are cutting the cake.

I remember the sense of relief I felt. We did it! Finally it was over! Physically, mentally and emotionally, we felt like we had completed something, and we had—a six-week engagement filled with so much activity that we hardly had time to rest.

Did we truly realize what we had done? Did we have a plan for making our marriage successful? Did we have any idea what type of commitment we had just made, and what it would mean? In reality, our wedding was not the completion of an engagement but *the beginning of a new life*. Yet we scarcely knew what that life would involve. There was so much we didn't know about this thing called marriage.

We started our life together with the same youthful idealism and presumption typical of so many other couples. I suppose we believed we really wouldn't face many problems. We learned the hard way that building a solid marriage requires commitment, sacrifice and *work*.

During our first year of marriage, for example, we lived in Boulder, Colorado where the winters are cold and electric blankets are standard equipment for survival. I can recall how both of us enjoyed sliding into those toasty-warm sheets after the electric blanket had done its duty and thawed them. For some strange reason, however, neither of us could remember to turn out all the lights before climbing into bed. We would snuggle in and Barbara would say, "Sweetheart, did you remember to turn out all the lights?"

So I would hop out of our cozy bed and run barefoot through the 55-degree apartment, turning off light after light (that Barbara had turned on). It didn't happen that often, so I didn't mind—until one night when I dropped into bed totally exhausted. Just as I slipped into the third stage of anesthesia, Barbara gave me a little poke and said, "Sweetheart, aren't you going to turn out the lights?"

I groaned, "Honey, why don't you turn out the lights tonight?"

Barbara replied, "I thought you would because my dad always turned out the lights."

Suddenly I was wide awake. It dawned on me why I had been suffering occasional minor frostbite for the past few months. And I shot back, "But I'm not your dad!"

Well, we stayed up a long time that night discussing expectations—what Barbara expected me to do because her father had always done it and what I expected her to do no matter who had always done it.

That was a relatively simple conflict to resolve. A more serious problem arose during that same year as the starry-eyed excitement of our honeymoon slowly wore off and we began to awaken to the reality of our lifetime commitment.

Barbara was not quiet when we spent time together; in fact, she talked more than I did. But when we went to any type of party or large group function, I was the life of the party while she followed me around the room and hardly said a thing.

I remember feeling trapped. She seemed like an appendage attached to my side. One of the reasons I was originally attracted to Barbara was because she seemed strong in areas where I was weak, and vice versa. We made a good team, but somehow those things that once attracted me to her didn't feel the same anymore. We were just so *different*.

Meanwhile, Barbara was feeling trapped as well, but we weren't single any more. We both lived in the same home. At one point Barbara went into the bathroom and locked herself in, thinking *What in the world am I going to do? I can't get away from this.*

This was an important fork in the road for our marriage. Each of us had to decide before God if we would accept each other in spite of our differences and imperfections. We had made that commitment standing before a pastor on September 2, 1972, but now the implications of that commitment were staring us in the face.

Fortunately we made the right decision—to accept each other by faith, knowing that God had called us together. For though we were not well prepared for marriage, one all-important truth governed our relationship from the beginning: We were both committed to walking with God and knowing His will for our lives, and that has made all the difference for us.

Now you are thinking of beginning that same journey. You are either engaged or seriously contemplating marriage, and you're excited about the possibility of spending the rest of your life with this special person. Yet if you're honest with yourself, you probably feel a twinge of apprehension as well.

No other human relationship can approach the potential for intimacy and oneness than can be found within the context of the marriage commitment. And yet no other relationship can bring with it as many adjustments, difficulties and even hurts. There's no way you can avoid these difficulties; each couple's journey is unique. But there is much you can do to *prepare* for that journey.

An engagement is not just a time of preparation for a wedding, but also preparation for a marriage. In simple terms, the goal of *Preparing for Marriage* is to help you make the most thorough, comprehensive and in-depth preparations possible. In fact, it includes the type of material Barbara and I wish we had known before our wedding.

Like any journey with the potential for great reward, there are difficulties and obstacles to overcome along the way. This workbook is designed to guide and prepare you to move through those challenges.

Here is what you can expect from completing this study:

- ♥ You will discover the joy of knowing your fiancé(e) and being known by your fiancé(e) at levels you never imagined.
- ♥ You will talk about things you never dreamed you would, but always knew you should.
- ♥ You will know, apply and experience God's Word as it relates to engagement and marriage.
- ♥ You will be confident, certain and secure in your decision to marry (or perhaps not to marry).
- ♥ You will practice and apply foundational skills you need to build your marriage.

- You will acquire essential communication and conflict resolution skills.
- You will come to understand the critical nature of core roles in marriage.
- You will learn about God's design for true sexual intimacy.
- You will, hopefully, connect with a mentor couple who can assist and counsel you as you prepare to begin your journey.

Because we are committed to your success, we have not chosen the easy road in developing this workbook. You will be asked some tough questions and you'll be given some tough advice. Your preconceptions about engagement, marriage, God and His Word will be well tested. And in the process, you will be challenged to draw back the curtain, allowing who you really are to shine through.

Completing this workbook requires a commitment. A commitment to make it a priority and schedule the time required. A commitment to complete the work with integrity and honesty. And most importantly, a commitment to seeing the process through when difficulties challenge you to bail out.

If this is your intention, take a moment now and sign the commitment box on the next page. It will serve as a tangible reminder to you and your fiancé(e) that you believe your future marriage is worth your very best effort in premarital counseling now.

Discovery, risk, challenge, intimacy, commitment, truth—all of these and more are what make marriage the most incredible journey you could ever imagine. Get ready to laugh. Get ready to cry. Get ready to learn. And get ready to experience the joy of a relationship unlike any you have ever experienced before.

—Dennis Rainey
FamilyLife

OUR commitment

I commit to completing this premarriage workbook thoroughly and honestly. I will do my best to complete the assignments. I will make certain that this process remains at the top of my priority list and schedule. And when the process is difficult, I will press on.

I undertake this pledge as a reflection of my commitment to my fiancé(e) and our future marriage.

_____ Date Sept. 24. 02

_____ Date 9-24-02

HOW TO USE THIS WORKBOOK

Format

Preparing for Marriage includes two primary components:

I. THE MAIN SESSIONS

In each of the six main sessions you will learn more about how to make a marriage work, then interact with your fiancé(e) to apply the material to your relationship. These sessions are contained in parts two and three of the workbook.

Here's what you will find in each session:

> **True North** is a statement of the biblical truth related to the topic you are covering.
>
> **Get the Picture** introduces the topic, providing opportunities to answer questions and complete activities that allow you to grasp the topic and understand why it is important for you.
>
> **Get the Truth** is the Bible discovery section of each chapter where you will examine and discuss biblical truths to learn God's principles on different aspects of marriage.
>
> **Navigating by True North: Truths to Chart Your Course** is a list of summary statements of the key principles from each session.
>
> **Couple's Project** is the interaction portion of the session. Each project includes the following sections:
>
> > **Get Real**: Questions to guide your discussion;
> >
> > **Get to the Heart of Your Marriage—Prayer**: An opportunity to pray together and experience a spiritual discipline that will be one of the keys to your growing marriage in the years to come;
> >
> > **Get Deeper**: Optional assignments for the highly motivated—those who want to go where no engaged couple has gone before;
> >
> > **Questions for Those Who Were Previously Married.**

In addition, several of the sessions include bonus projects designed to help you deepen your experience as you work through the course.

II. SPECIAL PROJECTS

These five projects will guide you through critical discussions and help you learn even more about each other. The special projects are scattered throughout the workbook. We recommend that you complete them in the order in which they appear in this book.

These projects include:

- The "Personal History Worksheet" includes dozens of questions designed to help you understand your past and share it with your fiancé(e).
- "Great Expectations" helps you understand the expectations you are bringing into marriage.
- "Evaluating Your Relationship" provides a framework to ask some challenging questions about your relationship.
- "A Decision-Making Guide" is designed to help you discern God's will for your relationship.
- The "Purity Covenant" provides an opportunity to commit yourselves to sexual purity before you are married.

In order to receive the most benefit from this study, we strongly recommend that each of you obtain a workbook.

We had a difficult time choosing a word to refer to the person you are thinking of marrying. To make it as easy as possible we have chosen the word, "fiancé(e)," as in "Meet with your fiancé(e) to discuss your answers." We realize this word may feel a bit strange if you haven't yet decided to become engaged, but we believe you'll be able to overlook that awkwardness as you complete the workbook.

The Value of a Mentor

Completing this workbook together as a couple will be a rich experience. But there's an even better alternative: The value of this study will increase exponentially when it is completed under the guidance of a *mentor*. This could be a pastor, a counselor, a layperson or even better, a lay couple. In fact, we have written a separate *Leader's Guide* that gives the instructions counselors or mentors will need to guide you through your premarital counseling.

You may have already arranged to meet with a pastor, counselor or married couple who will serve as mentors for this course. By giving you access to their lives and allowing you to ask questions, they can provide a model for how a satisfying marriage relationship can work. This mentoring relationship may have a greater impact on you than anything else you learn in this course.

If you have been planning to complete this workbook on your own, we encourage you to think of a godly couple whom you respect and who has been married at least five years. Take the initiative to ask them to mentor you through your premarital counseling. Give them a copy of the *Leader's Guide* and ask them to invest in your future marriage by sharing with you and your fiancé(e).

There are three possible options for completing each session of the workbook. Which one you use will depend on whether you are working with a mentor and how he or she desires to work through the material.

Option 1	Option 2	Option 3
Learning and discussing the material with a mentor	**Learning the material on your own, then discussing it with a mentor**	**Learning the material without a mentor**
1. Complete the first part of each session with your mentor, either as a couple or as part of a small group of couples.	1. Complete the first part individually.	1. Complete the first part individually.
2. Complete the Couple's Project with your fiancé(e).	2. Complete the Couple's Project with your fiancé(e).	2. Complete the Couple's Project with your fiancé(e).
3. Meet with mentor to discuss issues as needed.	3. Meet with mentor to discuss both parts.	

Time Required

To receive the maximum benefit from the workbook, we strongly suggest the following:

- Plan on beginning the course so that, if at all possible, the last session is completed a minimum of four weeks *prior* to the wedding date.
- Set aside two weeks for each main session. This will give you time to complete your assignments, meet together to complete the Couple's Projects, and process what you are learning and discovering. It will also give you time to make needed decisions and resolve any special issues between sessions.
- That means that this study should be started at least 16 weeks, or four months before the wedding date.

We estimate that each session should take about two hours to complete: An hour for each of you to complete "Get the Picture" and "Get the Truth" and another hour to complete the Couple's Project. Some sessions might take a little longer.

Set aside plenty of time to complete the Special Projects. These are a key part of the workbook and worth the effort! They also will give you plenty of topics for discussion.

Charting a Course by True North

Did you know that when you hold up a compass and the arrow points north, it's not really pointing to the north pole?

The north pole is the geographic top of the earth. It is a fixed position that never changes. That's why it is called "true north." And it is from this fixed position that mapmakers draw their maps.

A compass, on the other hand, does not point to true north. Rather, it points to a magnetic field that is roughly 1,300 miles away from the north pole. This is called "magnetic north."

Here's the point: Every pilot and every sea captain must make constant adjustments from what his *compass* says is north and what the *map* says is true north. Failing to make this adjustment of even a few degrees early in the journey could mean missing the destination by hundreds of miles.

True north versus magnetic north is a revealing metaphor for someone searching for truth in today's world. True north is the truth of God's Word: It is fixed; it is certain; it is absolute. It is to life and marriage what the geographic north pole is to a map of Earth.

Magnetic north, on the other hand, can be deceiving. The arrow on the compass is pointing to what the compass says is north. It feels right. It looks right. Yet the magnetic field pulling that needle is uncertain. It will not direct you to your desired destination.

In the world you will find many ideas about building a strong marriage, but most of those ideas cannot be trusted. In creating this workbook, our desire is to provide you a glimpse of what God's Word says about building a strong marriage. By navigating according to True North—God's Word—you can look at the map, consider your destination, talk about the alternatives and decide how you should navigate your journey.

Additional Suggested Resources

In several of the Couple's Projects there is a "Get Deeper" section that gives you additional activities to help you delve more deeply into your relationship. The "Get Deeper" sections suggest reading all or part of the following books:

> *Money Before Marriage*, Larry Burkett with Michael E. Taylor, Moody Press, 1991
>
> *Rocking the Roles*, Robert Lewis and William Hendricks, NavPress, 1991
>
> *The Tribute and The Promise*, Dennis Rainey with David Boehi, Thomas Nelson, 1994
>
> *Staying Close*, Dennis Rainey, Word Publishing, 1989
>
> *Intended for Pleasure*, Ed and Gaye Wheat, Fleming H. Revell Co., 1981

We suggest that you obtain these books before beginning the study. Perhaps your church or your pastor, counselor or mentor couple already have them available for you to borrow.

AFTER THE WEDDING

There are many resources available to you to aid you in continuing to build your marriage after you have recited your vows to one another. We would suggest becoming involved in a Bible study group or Sunday School class for young marrieds. In such a group you can develop lifelong friendships and accountability as you help each other build godly marriages.

FamilyLife has developed a number of Bible study materials to aid you in continuing to grow in your marriage relationship. The following is a list of studies available from your Christian bookstore or directly from FamilyLife.

The HomeBuilders Couples Series®

For use in small-group home Bible studies with approximately two-hour meeting times:

Building Teamwork in Your Marriage by Robert Lewis

Building Your Marriage by Dennis Rainey

Building Your Mate's Self-Esteem by Dennis and Barbara Rainey

Expressing Love in Your Marriage by Jerry and Sheryl Wunder and Dennis and Jill Eenigenburg

Growing Together in Christ by David Sunde

Life Choices for a Lasting Marriage by David Boehi

Managing Pressure in Your Marriage by Dennis Rainey and Robert Lewis

Mastering Money in Your Marriage by Ron Blue

Resolving Conflict in Your Marriage by Bob and Jan Horner

HomeBuilders Couples Series® Bible Study Electives

For Sunday School classes or Bible study groups with approximately one-hour meeting times:

Building Teamwork in Your Marriage by Robert Lewis

Building Your Marriage by Dennis Rainey

Building Your Mate's Self-Esteem (with optional video) by Dennis and Barbara Rainey

Growing Together in Christ by David Sunde

A Final Note

One of the riskiest, but most rewarding benefits of a marriage relationship is the exhilarating experience of knowing and being known, of revealing and having another person reveal themselves to you. However, dating and even engagement can work against this process.

Journalist Sydney Harris wrote in a light, yet truthful vein:

> One of the chief reasons so many marriages fail is that the functions of a date and a mate differ radically: that of a date is to be charming; that of a mate is to be responsible; and, unfortunately, the most charming individuals are not necessarily the most responsible, while the most responsible are just as often deficient in charm.

You may think you know your fiancé(e) better than anyone else on earth. *Preparing for Marriage* is designed to help you deepen that knowledge. You will discuss your past and how it affects you today, your expectations about marriage, your respective strengths and weaknesses and how they can make you into a team, and so much more.

Remember, you are moving toward a lifetime commitment. Whatever is concealed now *will* eventually be revealed. Take the time to enjoy this course and to enjoy each other as you complete it. In this workbook you will find truths that will provide a beacon of hope as you begin your life together. Remember, you've only just begun, and this study will help point you in the right direction!

Part One

Preparing
the
Groundwork

Personal History Worksheet

Name __GARETT CORN__ Age __25__

Fiancé(e)'s name __Jen KOVACH__ Age __22__

Current occupation __Electrician__

Length of employment at your current job __9 months__

Highest level of education completed __12__

Hobbies and interests __time w/ Jen.__

_____

Previously married? ☐ Yes ☒ No   How many times? _____

☐ Divorced   ☐ Widowed

How long have you been divorced or widowed? _____

Much of who you are today is a product of your past. You and your fiancé(e) have probably not attempted to conceal your background from each other. But you may not have taken the time needed to adequately examine how your past influences your future.

One of the most underestimated influences on your new marriage is your family. When most couples marry today they assume that their marriage is between two people who want to become one. In reality, it is two people and *two families* that are coming together to form a new merger. You will leave your father and mother so that you can cleave and become one. However, as you will see in the years ahead, your family's impact on your new family must not be minimized, but rather understood and planned for.

We estimate this project will take at least two hours to complete, but you will find the effort well worth it! As you complete this project, you'll uncover some treasures along the way that will enrich your current relationship. You'll also locate a few old rusty nails that if not properly handled could create wounds that will infect your future marriage.

Take your time and answer each question as thoroughly as possible, then meet with your fiancé(e) to share your answers. If you are meeting with a mentor, give him or her a copy of the completed questions before you meet together.

Special Instructions: We recommend that you complete this project before you begin the regular sessions. Also, you will discuss the Life Map section of this worksheet in the Session Three Couple's Project.

section one: your relationship history

Your Current Relationship Story

1. How we met

   I first seen Jeen at Church. But the first time I seen Jen was not the first time I met her. Her mother Invited me to A CookOut on MAY# 11th, That was the first time we met!

2. What attracted me to her/him

   Like I was sAying the first time I Seen Jen was AT Church (sATurday night prAyer) THAT WAS THE FIRST THIng that attracted me to her besides the fact that I thought She was So BEUTIFUL.

3. How long we have been dating

   WE DATED FOR 7 months been engaged for 7 months (6 months to go).

About Your Friendships

1. Friendships for me have generally been (check one)
   - ❏ Easy, like falling off a log
   - ☑ So-so, I can take 'em or leave 'em
   - ❏ A challenge, a lot of work but satisfying and rewarding
   - ❏ Discouraging, more pain than I bargained for
   - ❏ Absent, I've never really had a truly close friend

   Now share why you checked the box you did:

   I've had So mawny freinds, Some will always be my friend. Some will fade away

2. Who are two of your closest friends and what makes those relationships special?

Jen is probably my Closest friend that I've had or will ever had. Robbie - we've been through everything together

How long have they been your friends?

Jen only 18 months but it feels longer
Robbie Since elementary School.

3. What are three to five adjectives these friends would use to describe you?

Jen - Curing, Respectful, Trustworthy

Rob - always fun - open hearted -

4. Describe a serious dating relationship from the past. Briefly state how it began, progressed and ended.

Jessica malvaso - It started in 11th grade Prom night ended 95 Ocean City

5. Can you identify any patterns that seem to be present in your relationships with the opposite sex? (Examples: "My tendency is to fall hard and fast, then get hurt." or "I am generally the more committed one in a relationship.")

Usually I am the one that falls hard & fast and then gets hurt. And I am more Committed in the relationship

For Previously Married Only

1. If you are divorced, why did you get a divorce? What were your reasons for divorcing?

    _____

    _____

    _____

2. Have you sought reconciliation with your former spouse? If so, how? If not, why not?

    _____

    _____

    _____

3. Have you discussed with your pastor or counselor whether you are free to remarry from a biblical standpoint? Write down your conclusion.

    _____

    _____

    _____

4. Give three reasons you are confident you have gotten over your previous marriage and are ready to marry again.

    _____

    _____

    _____

5. Give three reasons you may be unsure.

    _____

    _____

    _____

section two: your family

Home Environment

1. What was your family's socioeconomic background as you were growing up? What is it now?

    Lower - middle Class

    middle Class

2. How would you describe the emotional environment of the home you grew up in?

    ~~love~~

3. Did you experience any type of abuse (physical, emotional, sexual) as you grew up? Explain.

    No

4. What traumatic, tragic events or financial hardships did your family experience?

    Parents Divorce,

5. As you look back over your family history, do you see any legacies that have been passed from one generation to the next? (For example, one family might pass on a tradition of trusting God in tough circumstances, while another family might pass on a tendency toward turning to alcohol to alleviate problems.)

Yes ·

Parents

1. What words would you use to describe your parents' marriage? Tell why you chose each descriptive word.

2. As parents, what did your mom and dad do well?

Dad	Mom

3. As parents, what do you wish they would have done differently?

Dad	Mom
	taught me never to give up.

4. Describe the most significant impact your parents have had on you (positive or negative).

Dad	Mom

5. What roles did your parents assume in the household?

    DAD worked mom worked

    Who was the leader in the marriage?

    DAD

    Who was the leader as a parent?

    DAD

    How did they make decisions?

6. Choose three to five adjectives to describe your relationship with your father and tell why you chose them.

_____

_____

_____

_____

_____

7. Choose three to five adjectives to describe your relationship with your mother and tell why you chose them.

STRong, Strong willed _____

_____

_____

_____

_____

8. In what ways are you like each of your parents?

_____

_____

_____

_____

_____

9. In what ways are you different?

_____

_____

_____

_____

_____

10. Are there any unresolved issues between you and your parents? Articulate them here if you can.

_____

_____

_____

_____

_____

11. How do your parents feel about your choice of a mate?

_____

_____

_____

Siblings and Other Relatives

1. Rate your relationship with each of your siblings:

	Distant			Close	
Sibling _____	1	2	3	4	5
Sibling _____	1	2	3	4	5
Sibling _____	1	2	3	4	5
Sibling _____	1	2	3	4	5
Sibling _____	1	2	3	4	5
Sibling _____	1	2	3	4	5

2. With what relatives do you have a special and unique relationship and what makes it unique (grandparents, aunts, uncles, cousins, etc.)?

_____

_____

_____

SECTION THREE:
YOUR SPIRITUAL JOURNEY

1. What kind of religious upbringing did you have?

   _____

   _____

   _____

2. What role does God play in your life today?

   _____

   _____

   _____

3. How certain are you that you are going to heaven when you
   die?
   ❑   Absolutely certain
   ❑   Sort of certain
   ❑   Not certain at all
   Why?

   _____

   _____

   _____

4. Describe your spiritual life over the past 10 years. What were
   the high points?

   _____

   _____

   _____

   _____

   _____

What were the low points?

_____

_____

_____

_____

_____

_____

What caused growth or prevented growth?

_____

_____

_____

_____

_____

_____

5. Check the areas of your life in which you find it difficult to trust God and give Him complete control of:

    ❑ Sex   ❑ Relationship   ❑ Self-confidence
    ❑ Thought life   w/parents   ❑ Anger
    ❑ Worry   ❑ Finances   ❑ My future
    ❑ Career   ❑ Decision making
    ❑ Critical spirit ❑ Relationships
    ❑ Other _____

6. How has your involvement in a local church helped you grow in your relationship with Christ and in your outreach to others?

    _____

    _____

    _____

section four: your Life map

If you were to draw out your life from birth to this day, you would have before you a map of sorts. It would show where you started, turns you've made along the way, rivers you've crossed, mountains you've climbed. It may even show where you drove off the road, suffered an accident, or maybe had a flat tire along the way.

This project is designed to help you draw that map—for your benefit and your fiancé(e)'s. You'll both get a bird's-eye view of the major milestones that have shaped how you view yourselves and the world around you. The insights you gain, into your own life and your fiancé(e)'s, will deepen your understanding and appreciation of your unique relationship.

Important Notes

1. This exercise is intended to give a summary view of your life. You will not be able to fit your whole life story into this project.
2. Complete your Life Map privately. Do not interact with your fiancé(e) as you work on it.
3. You will not interact as a couple upon completing this Life Map project. Keep your Life Map confidential until Session Three when you will use it in a communication exercise.

Milestones

Answer the following questions to help you identify the major milestones in your life. As you consider each period of your life, here are some topics to think about:

- Favorite teachers, coaches, Sunday School teachers, youth workers, others who shaped your view of yourself and the world;
- Family events and relationships: vacations, tragedies, moves, sibling relationships, secrets;

- Hobbies and interests, sports, activities (Scouts, piano, tennis, etc.);
- Best friends, dating relationships;
- Good and bad decisions you've made;
- Spiritual highs and spiritual lows;
- Goals accomplished and goals yet to be met;
- Jobs you've had.

BIRTH THROUGH ELEMENTARY SCHOOL
1. List at least three memories that you can vividly recall about this period of your life.

_____

_____

_____

JUNIOR HIGH THROUGH HIGH SCHOOL
2. List at least five events/circumstances/experiences that you think shaped your life during this period.

_____

_____

_____

_____

_____

POST-HIGH SCHOOL TO THE PRESENT
3. List at least five events/circumstances/experiences that you would consider "life-changing" from this period of your life.

_____

_____

_____

_____

_____

Milestones to Mile Markers
Now you are going to turn these milestones in your life into "mile markers" on your own Life Map. A mile marker tells you where you are, how far you've come and how far you have to go. Choose the

milestones from the first section that you would like to plot on your Life Map and plot them at the appropriate spot.

Use the sample Life Map on next page as a guide in developing your own. The following are key things to remember:

- This is not meant to be an exhaustive life history. It is meant to be a simple, clear overview of the major milestones in your life and how they affected you.
- The midline is emotional neutral. Anything above the midline indicates you found this to be a particularly enriching event/circumstance/experience. Anything below the midline indicates you found this to be a particularly difficult or troubling event/circumstance/experience.
- All of us have highs and lows in the normal ebb and flow of life. Points above and below the midline are not indicative of the value or quality of your life. They simply point out the major milestones of your life, how you view them and how they've influenced you.

(Try to plot *at least* seven and *no more than* 12 mile markers.)

Sample Life Map

	Lows					Midline			Highs	
	-5	-4	-3	-2	-1	+1	+2	+3	+4	+5
Birth										
Start school							X			
Liked school								X		
Move to new town				X						
Graduate from Elementary										
Start Junior High										
Hated Jr. Hi.			X							
Found a new best friend								X		
Accepted Jesus as Savior										X
Graduate Junior High								X		
Start High School						X				
Don't make school team				X						
Best friend dies in accident	X									
First love									X	
After school job								X		
Accepted at college								X		
Get scholarship						X				
Graduate High School									X	
Post High School						X				
Off to college									X	
Break up with H.S. love		X								
Fail college class		X								
New major							X			
Graduate									X	
First job								X		
First date								X		
Get laid off					X					
New job									X	
Get engaged										X
Present										

Your Life Map

	Lows					Midline			Highs	
	-5	-4	-3	-2	-1	+1	+2	+3	+4	+5
Birth										
Graduate from Elementary										
Start Junior High										
Graduate Junior High										
Start High School										
Graduate High School										
Post High School										
Present										

GReat expectations

Special Note
We recommend that you complete this project
before you begin the regular sessions.

Expectations are so basic that we often don't even recognize them, yet they influence our behavior every day—how we treat people, how we react to different situations.

Each of us brings a certain set of expectations, a mental picture of how we will live and behave and interact, into a marriage. These expectations range from the routine to the profound—from dividing household responsibilities to determining who will take spiritual leadership in the home.

Many of these expectations are not necessarily good or bad; it's just that your expectations may differ from those of your fiancé(e). The challenge for most engaged couples is identifying some of the expectations that may later lead to conflict in their relationship.

For example, H. Norman Wright notes in his book, *Communication: Key to Your Marriage*, that:

> *Too many couples enter marriage blinded by unrealistic expectations.* They believe the relationship should be characterized by a high level of continuous romantic love. As one young adult said, "I wanted marriage to fulfill all my desires. I needed security, someone to take care of me, intellectual stimulation, economic security immediately—but it just wasn't like that!" People are looking for something "magical" to happen in marriage. But magic doesn't make a marriage work: hard work does.[1]

Buried expectations can poison a relationship. Unresolved expectations often lead to demands, and demands lead to manipulation. One partner maneuvers the other to meet the expectation while the other tries to avoid it. Inevitably, this leads to isolation in marriage with two partners playing absurd but dangerous games in an attempt to establish control.

While many of your own expectations about marriage will inevitably remain buried until after you are married, there is great value in discussing some of them now. In the process you should learn how to deal with differing expectations so they will not cause disappointment and disillusionment in your relationship.

Illusion and Reality

Some of our expectations are based on a fantasy of romance and marriage that our culture often promotes. As an example of unrealistic expectations, a famous musician appeared on a television talk show a few years ago and was asked about his disastrous marriage several years earlier. He said he married because he was not willing to confront his addiction to drugs and alcohol. "I got married because I thought I would be happy," he said. "But I still put cocaine up my nose and I still drank a bottle of scotch every day. Nothing changed."

Like so many other people contemplating marriage, this musician had bought into the common illusion that marriage would solve all his problems. He thought that this relationship would give him so much happiness, peace and strength that his difficulties with alcohol and drugs would just melt away.

1. What do you think of each of the following statements?

   a. "These feelings of love and passion will never fade after we are married."

   b. "Life will continue to be exciting after we are married."

   c. "If I get married, I will no longer be lonely."

   d. "My mate will meet all my needs."

   e. "If I get married, I will be able to help my mate become a better person."

   f. "My marriage will be great because I'll marry a Christian."

Each of these statements contains a grain of truth, but these beliefs also could quickly lead to disappointment and disillusionment. Hard as it may be for you to believe, your feelings of love and passion *will* tone down a bit after marriage. Life will not always be exciting— remember that you're pledging to care for one another "in *sickness* and in health."

2. Do you think any of those statements about a fantasy marriage ring true for your relationship?

   _____

   _____

   _____

   _____

A Guiding Principle

As you begin to identify and discuss your expectations, Philippians 2:3,4 provides a principle that should govern your attitudes:

> Do nothing from selfishness or empty conceit, but with humility of mind let each of you regard one another as

more important than himself; do not merely look out for your own personal interests, but also for the interests of others.

1.   Complete the following statement:
      When one of my expectations is not met, I should...

_____

_____

_____

_____

The Christian life is ultimately "other" focused, not "me" focused. The aim of our lives is to meet the needs of others. That means our expectations, many of which are legitimate, must often be put aside for the needs of others. This is what Christ called "dying to self."

Discussing Expectations

Complete your Great Expectations Survey individually; then meet with your fiancé(e) to discuss your answers. Here are a few suggestions for your discussion:

- *Identify* where the expectation came from: Is this a product of my background, education, culture or personality?
- *Discuss* why the expectation is important to you and ways you can fulfill it in a nondemanding way.
- *Resolve* together how this expectation can be:
  - *Accepted* and met by your fiancé(e)/spouse;
  - *Adjusted* so that it is reasonable;
  - *Abandoned* as unrealistic.

This project can be like mining for precious ore. You may have to move tons of earth to get ounces of gold, but those priceless nuggets are well worth the effort it takes to find them. The same can be true of our expectations. Because many of our expectations are buried beneath a lifetime of conditioning, we must work to uncover them and that is just what this project will help you do.

You will be accomplishing two things as you complete this project. First, you will narrow the gaps in the number of areas where you have reasonable expectations. And secondly, you will eliminate some gaps alltogether as you identify unrealistic expectations that you need to release.

great expectations survey

Write down the specific expectations you have for your marriage in the following categories. Write down how *you feel* about the particular item, not what you think your fiancé(e) wants to hear. Answer all the questions. The more specific and honest you are, the more gold you'll discover.

Marriage Relationship

1. How will you make decisions once you are married?

   _____

   _____

   _____

   _____

   What will you do when you find you cannot agree?

   _____

   _____

   _____

   _____

2. When you are ill, how much sympathy and attention do you desire? What does being taken care of look and feel like to you?

   _____

   _____

   _____

   _____

3. How much time do you expect to spend with your friends after you are married?

   _____

   _____

   _____

4. How will you relate to opposite-sex friends after you are married?

_____

_____

_____

_____

Finances

1. Who will be the primary financial provider in the family?

_____

_____

_____

2. Do you anticipate both husband and wife pursuing careers? If yes, for how long?

_____

_____

_____

3. How will you decide on major purchases?

_____

_____

_____

_____

4. Who will pay the bills and keep the checkbook?

_____

_____

_____

5. What is your philosophy of giving (to your church or other charitable organizations) and how will you make decisions about giving?

_____

_____

_____

_____

6. What are your convictions about the use of credit cards?

    _____

    _____

    _____

    _____

Home

1. Where do you want to live?

    _____

    _____

    In what *setting* would you want to live (i.e., city, suburb, small town, rural, plains, mountains, desert, coastal, etc.)?

    _____

    _____

    _____

2. Will you live in an apartment or house? Will you rent or buy?

    _____

    _____

    _____

3. What do you expect your standard of living to look like after five years of marriage?

    _____

    _____

    _____

    _____

4. How soon after you are married do you expect to have your home reasonably furnished? What does "reasonably furnished" mean to you?

_____

_____

_____

_____

Housekeeping

1. Who will prepare each meal and what types of food will you eat?

_____

_____

_____

2. How important are family mealtimes to you? Why?

_____

_____

_____

_____

How often will you eat out?

_____

_____

3. How clean do you want your home to be? What does "clean" mean to you?

_____

_____

_____

_____

4. Who will do each of the following?
Laundry and ironing _____
Purchasing groceries _____
Automobile maintenance _____
Home repairs and yard work _____

General household cleaning _____
Cleaning bathrooms_____
Making the bed _____

5. Do you want a pet in the home? If so, what type?

    _____

    _____

    _____

Children and Parenting

1. What is your attitude toward children?

    _____

    _____

    _____

    _____

2. When will you begin having children and how many would you
    like to have?

    _____

    _____

3. What would you do if you cannot conceive children of your
    own?

    _____

    _____

    _____

    _____

4. What is your view on abortion?

    _____

    _____

    _____

    _____

5. What is your view on birth control?

_____

_____

_____

_____

6. Who will be the primary nurturer/caregiver of your children?

_____

_____

7. How will you discipline your children? How do you envision sharing that responsibility?

_____

_____

_____

_____

Social/Entertainment

1. How often do you want to invite people to your home?

_____

_____

_____

    What kind of entertaining do you expect to do (i.e., formal or informal dinner, lavish or simple parties, etc.)?

_____

_____

_____

2. How often will you go out on dates?

_____

3. What will be the role of television in your lives and what guidelines will you have?

    _____

    _____

    _____

    _____

    What about movies?

    _____

    _____

4. How will your personal friendships (his friends/her friends) change after marriage?

    _____

    _____

    _____

    _____

5. What hobbies or recreational pursuits will you pursue individually?

    _____

    _____

    _____

    _____

    Together?

    _____

    _____

    _____

    _____

    How *often* will you pursue them?

    _____

    _____

6. How do you feel about having alcoholic beverages in your home?

_____

_____

_____

Spiritual Life

1. Who will take spiritual leadership in the home and what do you think this means?

_____

_____

_____

_____

2. When and how often will you pray and study the Bible together?

_____

_____

_____

_____

3. Where will you attend church and what will your involvement be?

_____

_____

_____

_____

4. In what ways do you anticipate reaching out to others as a couple?

_____

_____

_____

_____

Holidays/Vacations/Special Occasions

1. Where will you spend Christmas, Thanksgiving and Easter?

    _____

    _____

    _____

    _____

    How will you decide?

    _____

    _____

    _____

    _____

2. What expectations do you have for celebrating holidays?

    _____

    _____

    _____

    _____

3. What will you do during your vacations?

    _____

    _____

    _____

    _____

4. How will you celebrate birthdays and wedding anniversaries?

    _____

    _____

    _____

    _____

5. How much will you spend on gifts for family, friends and each
other for...

	Your		
	Family	**Children**	**Friends**	**Each Other**
Birthdays?	_____	_____	_____	_____
Christmas?	_____	_____	_____	_____
Weddings?	_____	_____	_____	_____
Anniversaries?	_____	_____	_____	_____

6. How will you spend your weekends?

_____

_____

_____

Parents and Other Relatives

1. How do you think your relationship to your parents will change
after you are married?

_____

_____

_____

_____

2. How much time do you anticipate spending with your parents
and your in-laws?

_____

_____

_____

3. What other relatives do you expect to be involved in your marriage and family (siblings, aunts, uncles, cousins)? In what ways
would they be involved?

_____

_____

_____

_____

4. How involved do you want your parents and in-laws to be in your children's lives?

_____

_____

_____

_____

How will you accomplish this?

_____

_____

_____

_____

5. What type of relationship do you expect to have with your parents and your in-laws after marriage?

_____

_____

_____

_____

Sex

1. In your first year of marriage, how often do you expect to experience sexual intimacy?

_____

_____

_____

_____

2. What are your expectations about sex on your honeymoon?

_____

_____

_____

_____

3. What do you feel about your spouse at times saying no to having sex?

_____

_____

_____

_____

4. What about sex during the wife's menstrual cycle?

_____

_____

_____

_____

for those who have been previously married

Marriage

1. Review each category below and ask yourself this question:
    What unique expectations might I be holding on to from my
    previous marriage that I haven't yet discussed? Or to put it
    another way: What are areas of this marriage that I'm expect-
    ing to be different from my previous one?

    Marriage Relationship

    _____

    _____

    _____

    _____

    Finances

    _____

    _____

    _____

    _____

    Home

    _____

    _____

    _____

    _____

    Housekeeping

    _____

    _____

    _____

    _____

Children and Parenting

_____

_____

_____

_____

Social/Entertainment

_____

_____

_____

_____

Spiritual

_____

_____

_____

_____

Holidays/Vacations/Special Occasions

_____

_____

_____

_____

In-laws/Relatives

_____

_____

_____

_____

Sex

_____

_____

_____

_____

2. If your fiancé(e) needs to contact his or her former spouse (due to finances, business, in-laws, children, etc.) how do you want that to be handled?

_____

_____

_____

_____

Children
(If applicable)

1. What kind of relationship do you expect your new spouse to have with your children?

_____

_____

_____

_____

2. What kind of relationship do you expect to have with your spouse's children?

_____

_____

_____

_____

3. How will you handle the children's need to see your former in-laws—their grandparents, aunts, uncles and cousins?

_____

_____

_____

4. What guidelines need to be developed in disciplining the children?

_____

_____

_____

_____

5. How will you handle disagreements with former spouses about how to raise the children?

_____

_____

_____

_____

6. What are the financial burdens involved in raising the children? How will these be handled?

_____

_____

_____

_____

7. Will you have additional children? When? How many?

_____

_____

_____

_____

1. H. Norman Wright, *Communication: Key to Your Marriage*, (Ventura, Calif.; Regal Books, 1974) from the Introduction.

Part Two

Laying the foundation

The men that women marry, and why they marry them,
will always be a marvel and a mystery to the world.
—HENRY WADSWORTH LONGFELLOW

Why marriage?

true North

Marriage is God's idea

Why Are You Considering Marriage?

That may sound like a simple question, yet how you answer it may give you a strong indication of how much you know about this commitment you're considering.

Seneca, a Roman philosopher, once wrote, "You must know for which harbor you are headed if you are to catch the right wind to get you there." The problem in our culture today is that, when it comes to marriage, many couples choose to set sail for the wrong harbors:

- *The harbor of idealism*—"If I get married, I'll be happy until the end of my days."

- *The harbor of companionship*—"I can't stand the thought of living alone for the rest of my life."
- *The harbor of sexual fulfillment*—"Marriage means that I can enjoy sex anytime I want and never feel guilty or fearful."
- *The harbor of social acceptance*—"My family and friends keep asking me, 'When are you going to settle down and get married?'"

Determining which harbor you *should* head for is the first and most important decision you should make as you consider marriage.

get the picture

Read the following case study, then answer the questions that follow.

Case Study: The Story of Bob and Sherry

ACT ONE: THE MAGICAL MEETING

Who would have ever thought that Bob, an athlete and outdoorsman, and Sherry, a refined southern lady, would wind up falling in love? They met at a singles ski retreat deep in the heart of the Rocky Mountains of Colorado. The moment Bob saw Sherry, he approached her and asked her out. Sherry was intrigued that someone would be so bold, and she agreed.

For the rest of the week they found themselves enthralled with each other's company. They skied together, dined together, sipped hot chocolate together and talked about everything they could think of. It all felt so natural, so easy, like they actually fit together.

Both Bob and Sherry had dated many others in the past, but somehow they knew this relationship was different. After the retreat, they each returned to their homes, 200 miles apart. Bob co-owned a landscaping company and Sherry sold pharmaceuticals. But over the next few months they gave the telephone company plenty of financial support. They spent hours talking about their lives and their feelings for one another. They wrote each other regularly and often sent creative gifts. Over the next few months they spent as much time together as they could.

ACT TWO: GETTING SERIOUS

It was natural for Bob and Sherry to begin thinking about marriage. He was 28 and she was 26, and they had both felt now was the time to settle down.

Bob believed that the most important thing to know before he got married was that his future bride would be compatible with him. He wanted to find someone who was attractive and fun to be with. He also desired a wife who enjoyed fishing, was willing to give him the freedom to be with his buddies, could cook and keep the house clean.

Sherry also had expectations about marriage and her future spouse. She dreamed of marriage as a wonderful romantic adventure with the man she loved. He would be sensitive, attractive, well organized and willing to share the home responsibilities. He would express his feelings, be a good listener and provide security. He would enjoy children as much as she did and would make a loving, caring father.

Because they had strong feelings for each other, Bob and Sherry were more than willing during the dating relationship to please each other. Bob often would be very vulnerable when he talked with Sherry, telling her about his struggles and doubts as well as his victories. He was the supreme gentleman, very creative with his romantic gestures, and he really cared about listening to what Sherry had to say. He even took her to the theater, which she loved. Sherry thought, *This is the man of my dreams. We're perfect for each other.*

Sherry had never gone fishing as a child, but now she found herself spending weekends at a lake, casting for bass with Bob. She would attend his softball games and even cheered for Bob's favorite basketball team on television. Everything seemed fun when they spent time together. And Bob could not believe his taste buds when he ate Sherry's cooking. He thought, *This woman is like me in so many ways and she likes to do things for me*.

Of course, no two people are alike and that was the case with Bob and Sherry. Their families were quite different—Bob's dad was an auto mechanic and his mother a waitress. Sherry's parents were divorced, but her father, a wealthy attorney, provided well for all of them. This wide gap in socioeconomic background was most apparent in the uneasiness they felt when they visited their prospective in-laws.

Bob was a boisterous, outgoing man who loved to be around lots of people. Sherry was much more reserved; she enjoyed spending time with a few close friends, but felt uncomfortable at a large party. She loved reading while he watched television to relax.

Sherry was bothered a bit about the difference in their religious convictions. She attended her church regularly; her belief in God was important to her. Bob said he had never enjoyed church and didn't attend on his own. But he did seem to enjoy going with her when he visited on weekends. That gave Sherry hope that he would eventually change. *Considering everything, we seem perfect for each other*, she thought.

They were tired of being single and they wanted to start a family. And the fact was they just couldn't stand to be apart. They couldn't imagine spending life without each other. So five months after they met, they decided to marry.

They were engaged four months—just enough time to arrange the wedding. The final weeks were hectic, with last minute preparations and many frazzled nerves, but the big day finally arrived. The ceremony went by in a blur, and suddenly they found themselves reciting their vows: "until death do we part."

They headed off on their honeymoon to live happily ever after.

1. What do you think about Bob and Sherry's decision to get married? Is it wise, or not? Why?

    _____

    _____

    _____

    _____

2. If Bob and Sherry had approached you and asked, "Do you think we are ready to get married?" how would you answer?

    _____

    _____

    _____

    _____

3. What are their reasons for getting married? Are they valid reasons? Why or why not?

    _____

    _____

    _____

    _____

ꝶet tHe tRutH

Actually, Bob and Sherry may well be a superb match, but their decision to marry may be a bit hasty. So far they have known each other a total of six months, and most of that time has been spent 200 miles apart. They are so caught up in a whirlwind of emotions that they have failed to work out some crucial issues before they commit their lives to each other.

For one thing, there is much they still do not know about each other. Their family backgrounds are quite different and the fact that Sherry's parents were divorced means that she grew up without a good model of how to build a successful marriage. They also have not really discussed philosophical or religious viewpoints to assess their compatability on some of the deeper issues of life. Their expectations about marriage are different. In fact, they seem to have different goals in mind as they approach marriage.

In a sense, they are beginning marriage in the dark. And that's common of many couples today. Writer Barbara Dafoe Whitehead once commented, "It took humans many centuries to work out a cultural institution—called marriage—capable of linking men and women in mutual acceptance, loyalty and cooperation." That sounds logical, until you remember a key fact: Marriage was not designed by humans but by God at the inception of the human race.

In this session you will discover that as you set sail in your marriage, the only safe, secure and sensible harbor is the one found in the Person and the Word of God. God intended marriage to be much more than a convenient pairing of a man and a woman. To find the answer to the question "Why marriage?" we must go back to marriage's origin—back to the book of beginnings, the book of Genesis. It is there that we will discover God's purpose and plan for marriage.

Purpose Number One: Mutually Completing One Another

In the second chapter of Genesis we pick up the creation story after God has created man: "Then the LORD God said, 'It is not good for the man to be alone; I will make him a helper suitable for him' " (Genesis 2:18).

Up to this point in creation, God had said everything was good. Yet here, by God's own declaration, we see that something is not good. In fact, God declared that Adam's singleness was the opposite of good.

1.   Why do you think it wasn't good for Adam to be alone?

_____

_____

_____

_____

In the garden Adam walked and talked with God. Yet that was not enough. God chose to create a unique need—aloneness—in Adam that was not filled by His personal presence. Adam experienced God in the midst of perfection, yet Adam was *alone*.

2. Continue reading in Genesis to see what God did to solve Adam's problem:

> "And out of the ground the LORD God formed every beast of the field and every bird of the sky, and brought them to the man to see what he would call them; and whatever the man called a living creature, that was its name. And the man gave names to all the cattle, and to the birds of the sky, and to every beast of the field, but for Adam there was not found a helper suitable for him. So the LORD God caused a deep sleep to fall upon the man, and he slept; then He took one of his ribs, and closed up the flesh at that place. And the LORD God fashioned into a woman the rib which He had taken from the man, and brought her to the man" (Genesis 2:19-22).

a. Why do you think Adam could not find a suitable helper?
    ❑ None of the animals understood football.
    ❑ Adam snorted like a buffalo, but he couldn't keep up with the herd.
    ❑ Adam was interested in the gorilla, but her breath could peel a banana.
    ❑ Like many men, Adam was keeping his options open.
    ❑ God was showing Adam his need for a mate.
    ❑ Other_____

b. What did God do to address Adam's need for companionship?

    _____

    _____

    _____

God's solution for Adam's need was to "make him a helper suitable for him." It's important here to note that "helper" does not mean "servant." On the contrary, in the day when Moses penned these words, to identify a woman as a helper was counter to the culture's common low view of women. He actually elevated the sense of a woman's worth and role by calling her by the same name used to describe God Himself other places in the Old Testament (see Psalm 30:10 and 54:4). To be called a "helper" here speaks more to the simple fact that God had plans for Adam that he could not fulfill without a mate—he was *incomplete*. Adam needed Eve.

Also notice that this passage does not imply that every unmarried person is incomplete without a mate. All of us are created in the image of God and bring glory to God when we yield ourselves to His purpose and plan for our lives. Jesus, after all, was single. However, in God's timing He does sovereignly choose to bring a husband and wife together for them to accomplish together what they couldn't have accomplished separately.

When God calls you to marry, He gives you a mate who, by divine design, will complete you. Together you will be stronger and more effective than if you remain single. Most happily married couples could point to specific examples of how God has fit them together. For example:

- The husband is people-oriented, and his wife is task-oriented (or vice versa). He helps her relate socially to others while she keeps him focused on tasks they need to complete.
- He races through life at a fast pace, while her inner clock impels her to move much slower. He helps her make it on time to meetings while she helps him stop and smell the roses.

  In His wisdom God brings two people together to balance each other out, to fill each other's gaps. They are stronger as a team than they were as individuals. They are two *independent* people who choose to become *interdependent*.

3. As you look at your relationship with your fiancé(e), in what ways are you...

Alike	Different
_____	_____
_____	_____
_____	_____
_____	_____
_____	_____
_____	_____

4.   Describe some ways that your differences and weaknesses make you stronger as an *interdependent team*.

_____

_____

_____

_____

5.   If a couple does not see their differences as part of God's design and purpose for their marriage, how will those differences challenge their relationship over time?

_____

_____

_____

_____

It is your commitment to God—to know Him, grow in your relationship with Him and obey Him—that will enable you to see your spouse as the perfect complement to your life.

Purpose Number Two: Multiplying a Godly Legacy

As we continue looking at the book of Genesis, we find the second purpose of marriage: "And God blessed them; and God said to them, 'Be fruitful and multiply, and fill the earth'" (Genesis 1:28).

6.   This passage makes it clear that, according to God's design for marriage, having children is not an option, but a command. What do you think God had in mind when He made bearing children such a priority?

_____

_____

_____

_____

7. What do the following passages from Psalms tell us about God's opinion of children and why they are important to Him?

    "Behold, children are a gift of the LORD; the fruit of the womb is a reward. Like arrows in the hand of a warrior, so are the children of one's youth. How blessed is the man whose quiver is full of them; they shall not be ashamed, when they speak with their enemies in the gate" (Psalm 127:3-5).

    "For He established a testimony in Jacob, and appointed a law in Israel, which He commanded our fathers, that they should teach them to their children, that the generation to come might know, even the children yet to be born, that they may arise and tell them to their children, that they should put their confidence in God, and not forget the works of God, but keep His commandments" (Psalm 78:5-7).

    _____

    _____

    _____

    _____

    Not only is having children a reward and blessing (see Psalm 127:3-5), but it also has an essential part in God's plan to pass on His Word to the next generation. Although not every couple is able to have biological children of their own, it is God's intent for every couple to be ministering into the next generation— passing on their faith in God so the next generation can in turn pass it on to the next. Psalm 78 makes it clear that the family is one of the best environments in which this can happen.

8. God could use any method He wanted to tell people about Himself (see Numbers 22:21-33 and Luke 19:40). So why do you think He places such great emphasis on fathers and mothers passing on the truth about God to their children?

_____

_____

_____

_____

_____

God's original plan called for the home to be a "greenhouse"—a nurturing center where children grow up to learn character, values and integrity. In no other setting does a child learn more about how to live and how to relate to God than in a family.

Purpose Number Three: Mirroring God's Image

Consider God's purpose in creating humans:

> "Let Us make man in Our image, according to Our likeness; and let them rule over the fish of the sea and over the birds of the sky and over the cattle and over all the earth, and over every creeping thing that creeps on the earth." And God created man in His own image, in the image of God He created him; male and female He created them (Genesis 1:26,27).

This third purpose for marriage—that God created us to mirror His image—is a critical foundation for understanding God's design. It means that God chose to reveal to us a part of His character and being through our relationships.

For example, when we love one another we reflect God who created love and relationships. When we forgive each other, we reflect Him who forgave us in Christ (see Ephesians 4:32).

Why is this important? Because God created us to know Him and to live within the context of His plan for our lives. When a man and woman come together in a marriage with God at the center of their relationship, they will reflect His image. The world will see in that relationship a representation of who God is and how He loves.

Mysteriously, God chose to use a husband and wife to represent, or mirror, Him to humankind. It is through this marriage relationship that a couple *can* demonstrate a portion of God's love, forgiveness and long-suffering commitment to people.

9. List some ways that your marriage can mirror God's image. Sample answers are provided to spark your thinking.

We mirror God's...	To each other	To others
Perfect love	*when we believe the best about each other.*	*when we accept people as they are in spite of their weaknesses and faults.*
Commitment		
Forgiveness		
Unity (Father, Son, Holy Spirit)		

Summary

Marriage is far more than a cultural institution or an arrangement for a man and woman to meet their needs for companionship. As we consider the purposes of marriage we find the answers in the authoritative best-seller of all time, the Bible. All three of these purposes for marriage point us back to the spiritual originator of marriage—God. As Psalm 127:1 tells us, "Unless the LORD builds the house, they labor in vain who build it."

That means marriage is far more important than you may have thought. There is more at stake in your marriage than just two people trying to meet one another's needs. God's reputation—His image—is at stake in your marriage. To build a marriage according to God's design, you cannot ignore the spiritual foundation. In the next session, you'll learn more about that foundation.

NAVIGATING BY TRUE NORTH

TRUTHS TO CHART YOUR COURSE

- It's important to know why you are getting married.
- God created marriage so that two people would become one to:
  —Mirror His image;
  —Mutually complete one another;
  —Multiply a godly heritage.
- You complete each other through your unique differences and weaknesses.
- The family is a greenhouse for spiritual growth and a relay center for passing on spiritual truths to the next generation.
- In marriage the world sees a picture of what God is like.

Couple's Project

 ## get real

Interact as a couple on the following activities:

1. Spend a few minutes sharing and discussing your answers to the questions in the "Get the Picture" and "Get the Truth" sections. Be sure to ask your fiancé(e) to explain his or her answers.

2. Is the idea that your marriage would be a "mirror of God's image" a new one to you? How does this knowledge affect your concept of your future marriage?

_____

_____

_____

_____

_____

_____

3. Have you seen your relationship reflect God's glory to other people? If so, how?

_____

_____

_____

_____

_____

_____

4. In light of Scripture, has your view of having and raising children changed? If so, how?

_____

_____

_____

_____

If you have not fully discussed your thoughts about raising a family, this would be a good time.

a.　When do you want to begin having children?

_____

_____

b.　How many children do you think you would like to have?

_____

_____

c.　Do you feel ready to have children soon? Why or why not?

_____

_____

_____

_____

5.　Write a brief statement about the most important insights you have gained about God's purposes for marriage from this session. Share your statements with each other.

_____

_____

_____

_____

_____

get to the Heart of your marriage—prayer

One of the most practical ways to express your commitment to and dependence on God is to pray. Take a moment now and pray together telling God what place you want Him to have in your marriage. If you are not comfortable praying together, use the following suggested outline:

1. If you are in a place where you can do so, get on your knees, side by side. Getting on your knees is simply one way to physically show yourself humbled before God. Remember, it doesn't matter whether you're standing, sitting, driving in your car, walking, running or riding a bike—you can pray anytime, anywhere and in any position.

2. The following prayer is a suggestion for you to begin:

> Dear God,
> We bow before You to acknowledge that You are the creator of marriage. It is a divine institution designed to fulfill Your purposes. _____Fiancé(e)'s name_____ and I want You to be the center of our marriage. Because You created marriage, You are the One whom we want to look to for instruction, guidance and encouragement. We ask You to continue using Your Word to teach us how to build our marriage. In Christ's name, amen.

3. If there are other items you would like to pray about, feel free to continue your time of prayer together.

get Deeper

Here are two special optional assignments for those who want to go deeper.

1. Read chapter 11 in *Staying Close* by Dennis Rainey. This resource is available through FamilyLife at 1-800-FL-TODAY.

2. Complete the "Parental Wisdom Project" at the end of this session.

questions for those who were previously married

1. Refer to your Personal History Worksheet (on page 19) and discuss your answers to the questions for previously married in "Section One: Your Relationship History."

2. In what ways did your previous marriage fail to fulfill God's purposes for marriage?
   Mutually completing one another:

   _____

   _____

   _____

   Multiplying a godly legacy:

   _____

   _____

   _____

   Mirroring God's image:

   _____

   _____

   _____

3. If you were divorced: As you look back now, what mistakes did *you* make that led to the split? In other words, what was *your* responsibility?

   _____

   _____

   _____

   _____

4. If either of you have children, rate their emotional receptivity to the idea of your remarrying and explain why you think your child thinks the way he or she does:

	Negative			Positive	
	1	2	3	4	5

(child's name)

Why?_____

_____

	Negative			Positive	
	1	2	3	4	5

(child's name)

Why?_____

_____

	Negative			Positive	
	1	2	3	4	5

(child's name)

Why?_____

_____

	Negative			Positive	
	1	2	3	4	5

(child's name)

Why?_____

_____

5. What plans do you have for helping your children adjust to a potential new stepparent (and stepbrothers and/or stepsisters?

_____

_____

_____

_____

_____

_____

_____

a special message for those who were previously married

God's purposes for marriage, that you discovered in this session, point to the fact that God intends marriage to be a lifelong commitment between one man and one woman.

- Mutually completing one another involves becoming one flesh and experiencing oneness that is never to be divided. (You'll learn more about this in the next session.)
- Multiplying a godly legacy—having and raising children—is meant to be done in the context of a family with both parents present and involved.
- Mirroring God's image means mirroring the unity displayed in the Trinity. Father, Son and Holy Spirit never sever their relationship with one another.

If you are divorced, you need to make every effort to restore your relationship with your former spouse. We recognize there are extenuating circumstances in certain cases that can make this improbable and possibly unwise. You must seek godly counsel to help you sort through your unique issues.

As you consider another marriage, we assume that you have clear biblical grounds for your divorce. This means you have studied the biblical passages pertaining to divorce and have sought and *accepted* godly counsel. God *allows* divorce between a husband and wife in certain situations, but He never prescribes it. You need to have a clear conscience that you are living under His allowance and have the freedom, biblically, to remarry.

BONUS

PARENTAL
WISDOM PROJECT

"My son, observe the commandment of your father,
And do not forsake the teaching of your mother."

(PROVERBS 6:20)

"Honor your father and your mother, that your days
may be prolonged in the land which the
LORD *your God gives you."*

(EXODUS 20:12)

This project is designed to help you accomplish two things.

First, it will help you honor your parents by seeking their advice and counsel. The process of asking your parents these questions also offers you insight and wisdom from those who know you best (or at least the longest!). Keep in mind that as an adult, you are responsible for your own decisions in life. You are not asking your parents to make the decision about getting married. You are simply gaining their input, insights and counsel.

Second, it will help you honor your future in-laws by involving them in the process of helping you understand how to love their son or daughter. Your relationship with your in-laws can be one of the richest in your life when you begin your marriage by honoring them.

Instructions:

You have three options for completing this project. Choose the one that best fits your situation.

> **Option A:** Send the questionnaire to your parents and to your future in-laws along with a stamped return envelope. Include a cover letter explaining the project. Indicate that you need them to return their answers to you within one week of receiving it.

SAMPLE COVER LETTER

Dear _____,

_____[Fiancé(e)'s name]_____ and I are in our second week of premarital counseling and we are learning more about each other and marriage than we ever anticipated! We are as excited as ever about getting married.

One of our assignments is the enclosed "Parental Wisdom Questionnaire." We value your input. Would you complete these questions together and send your answers back to me by next week?

If there is something you don't think you can answer, just leave it blank. Or if you've got questions, give me a call.

We look forward to hearing your wisdom!

I love you,

_____

> **Option B:** Set aside a time when you can call your parents and your in-laws to go through the questionnaire over the phone. Be sure to give them ample time to think about their answers. You may want to send them the questions beforehand so they can think about and discuss their answers.

> **Option C:** Arrange to have a meal, dessert or coffee with your parents to go through the questionnaire. Let them know the questions beforehand so they can be thinking about their answers. Ask your parents their questions first, then your fiancé(e) can ask his or her in-law questions. If the interview is done in person, you may want to record their responses.

This project will take a little time to implement so get started soon. Stamp the envelope, make the phone call and set up the time to get together *now*!

SPECIAL INSTRUCTIONS
Please read the following before starting this project!
1. We do *not* recommend doing this project if you are *not* engaged.
2. If your parents or in-laws are divorced, talk over with your fiancé(e) how you should proceed. You may want to ask these questions of stepparents if you have a strong relationship, or you may want to only ask your biological parents. We believe, the more parents involved in this project, the better. However, you must decide what is appropriate and best for you at this time.
3. Feel free to eliminate or adapt the questionnaire if you sense that certain questions may be difficult or awkward for a parent to answer.
4. We understand that many who marry today come from difficult family backgrounds. The tragic consequences of alcoholism, abuse, neglect and alienation follow many young people into their marriages. If this is your situation, you may decide it is not appropriate to complete this project.

Whatever your relationship with your parents, God's Word calls you to honor them. A very helpful resource that can give you perspective and hope is *The Tribute and the Promise*, by Dennis Rainey (Thomas Nelson, 1994). Dennis provides some helpful insights and practical examples for those from difficult family backgrounds.

parental wisdom questionnaire

Answer the following questions as if your child is asking them:

1. What *strengths* do you see in my life that will help me in marriage?

    _____

    _____

    _____

    _____

    _____

    _____

2. What *weaknesses* do you see in my life that will be a challenge for me to work on and overcome in my marriage?

    _____

    _____

    _____

    _____

    _____

    _____

3. If you could give me one piece of advice about marriage (based on what you did right or did wrong), what would it be and why?

    _____

    _____

    _____

    _____

    _____

    _____

4. What is your best advice to me in the following areas as I embark on this new adventure called marriage? Pick three to five that you would like to comment on.

    ♥ Finances

    ♥ Communication

    ♥ Sex

    ♥ Husband/Wife roles

    ♥ Commitment

    ♥ Humor

    ♥ Parenting

    ♥ Spiritual growth

    ♥ Priorities in life

    ♥ Work

    ♥ Other

5. If you could keep just one memory, experience or time together in all your married life, what would it be and why?

    _____

    _____

    _____

    _____

    _____

    _____

    _____

6. Is there anything special or meaningful to you that you would like us to include in the wedding ceremony?

_____

_____

_____

_____

7. How do you anticipate my relationship with you, as my parents, will change now that I am marrying and establishing a new family and home?

_____

_____

_____

_____

8. How would you like us to handle holidays?

_____

_____

_____

_____

9. If God gives us children, how involved would you like to be in their lives?

_____

_____

_____

_____

10. Would you like us to drop in unannounced or call before visiting?

_____

_____

_____

_____

11. Do you have any specific expectations about where we will attend church?

_____

_____

_____

_____

Answer the following questions as if your future son-in-law or daughter in-law is asking them:

1. What are some qualities you see in me, or know about me, that make you think I am the right person for your son/daughter to marry?

_____

_____

_____

_____

_____

_____

_____

2. What unique and personal advice would you give me about your son/daughter that will help me be the life partner he/she needs?

_____

_____

_____

_____

_____

_____

3. What would you like me to call you after we are married?

_____

_____

"There is no more lovely, friendly, and charming
relationship, communion or company than
a good marriage."

—Martin Luther

God's equation for marriage:
When One plus One equals One

true North

GOD'S PLAN FOR MARRIAGE
INVOLVES FOUR COMMITMENTS THAT
ARE LIVED OUT OVER A LIFETIME
IN THE POWER OF THE HOLY SPIRIT:
RECEIVING, LEAVING, CLEAVING
AND BECOMING ONE FLESH.

For thousands of years, rulers and wealthy landowners built huge castles as homes for protection from enemies. Over the years, however, those enemies devised many ingenious methods of piercing a castle's defenses. They built catapults to hurl stones against the walls or over them. They used battering rams to break through a wall. They constructed towers on wheels, then moved the towers up to the castle wall to allow men to breach the walls.

And if none of those strategies worked, they turned to the siege. They surrounded the castle and prevented food, water and any other supplies from entering. After weeks and sometimes months, the castle's inhabitants were forced to surrender.

By the thirteenth century in England, castle designers had learned from the mistakes of previous generations. They included many ingenious defenses in their blueprints:

- The outer walls angled sharply outward at the bottom. This provided additional stability and also provided a defensive strategy: huge boulders dropped by castle defenders would bounce off the sloped bottom and hit the enemy.
- Arrow slits were installed in the walls and designed so that archers could aim their bows.
- Slots were left at the top of the outer walls so they could create "hoardings"—wooden structures that hung out beyond the walls that allowed defenders to aim straight down at the enemy.
- Huge storage areas were created to accumulate food that could sustain inhabitants of the fortress for months at a time.
- A well was dug within the inner ring of walls so that castle defenders would have an independent water supply.

As you seriously consider marriage, you should realize that you will be constructing a home that needs to withstand the catapults and battering rams of our twenty-first-century culture. To build a strong marriage and family you and your fiancé(e) need to build your marriage from the same, proven blueprints.

get the picture

Read the following case study, then answer the questions that follow:

The Continuing Saga of Bob and Sherry

Sherry was too exhausted for much sexual intimacy on their wedding night and Bob was understanding. Then, the next morning, she awoke with a stomach flu. They somehow made it to their honeymoon location, but Sherry spent three full days in bed. Bob found himself walking alone along a warm, romantic beach, wondering why he was even there and whether this was some sort of omen of trouble to come.

Fortunately Sherry recovered fully, and they were able to enjoy at least a few days of romance and intimacy. Within a few weeks of returning home and settling into their new lives, however, they began experiencing some tension.

Sherry was unhappy with her new job in a new city. A successful pharmaceuticals salesman back home, now she found herself starting from scratch again, building up a customer base and digging for referrals. She would arrive home exhausted and irritable. On top of that, Bob had expected her to earn more money—something closer to her salary before they were married. Now their finances were tighter than he wished.

Bob had always worked long hours, often not returning home until late in the evening. With Sherry living in another town during their engagement, this never mattered. Now, Sherry felt lonely in a new home. "I hardly know anybody here," she complained. Bob, meanwhile, felt Sherry didn't understand his need to work long hours in order to keep up with their seasonal workload at the landscaping company. "It won't be as bad during the winter," he explained.

What bothered Bob and Sherry most, however, were the changes they saw in each other after their marriage.

It was as if, once they had reached their goal of finding a mate, they relaxed and didn't work as hard on the relationship. They didn't talk like they once did, and they argued more.

Bob planned a special surprise fishing trip one weekend, and was stunned when Sherry announced, "I really don't like fishing. Can't we do something else instead?" When Bob said he would go with a friend instead, Sherry angrily asked, "What do you expect me to do all weekend—polish our silverware?" The following week, she was just as surprised when she told Bob about a theatrical play she wanted to see, and he replied that he would rather just stay home and watch a movie on their VCR!

They clashed with each other on a number of fronts—how they divided housework, the way they kept track of their finances, how they treated their in-laws, and so on.

Perhaps, they thought, *we really aren't compatible after all. Perhaps we have just made a big mistake.*

1. Why do you think Bob and Sherry became disillusioned so quickly after marriage?

    _____

    _____

    _____

    _____

    _____

2. What could they have done *before* they were married to make the transition easier?

    _____

    _____

    _____

    _____

ϱet the truth

If you were to describe the world's blueprints for marriage, it probably would be titled "The 50/50 Marriage." This is how most people think of marriage and on the surface it sounds reasonable: "If I do my part, and he does his, we'll meet each other halfway."

This plan is destined for failure, however, because...

* It does not take unreal expectations into account.
* It is impossible to know when your mate has met you halfway.
* It fails to anticipate the natural selfishness you both bring into a relationship.

Fortunately, the Bible offers a better plan. Let's revisit the book of Genesis, where we will examine four commitments essential to building a marriage according to God's blueprints. Although the biblical principles for marriage are thousands of years old, we will discover that they are time-tested and relevant for our marriages today.

Commitment Number One: Receive Your Mate

In Genesis 2:21-25, we read:

> So the LORD God caused a deep sleep to fall upon the man, and he slept; then He took one of his ribs, and closed up the flesh at that place. And the LORD God fashioned into a woman the rib which He had taken from the man, and brought her to the man. And the man said, "This is now bone of my bones, and flesh of my flesh; she shall be called Woman, because she was taken out of Man."

Once God had made Adam "a helper suitable for him" (Genesis 2:18) one question remained: What would be Adam's response? Remember, he had been busy naming the animals when God used some celestial Sominex to put him under for rib surgery. No doubt, he had been dreaming of lions, tigers and bears, yet now before him was God's custom-made helper.

93

1. Put a check by everything that Adam *knew* about Eve when he first laid eyes on her:

   ❑ She could cook like his mom.
   ❑ One day she would inherit five million shares of Microsoft.
   ❑ Her voice reminded him of some feathery thing he named "bird."
   ❑ She really knew how to kiss.
   ❑ She liked to rent new-release movies (no black and white oldies).
   ❑ Other _____

No, Adam didn't know anything about Eve except that she had come from God.

2. So how did he respond?

   _____

   _____

   "This is now bone of my bones and flesh of my flesh; she shall be called Woman, for she was taken out of Man" (Genesis 2:23).

The Living Bible paraphrase comes closest to capturing the real spirit of Adam's response: "This is it!" Another way to interpret the exclamation is "Wow! Where have you been all my life?" In other words, Adam was excited—he was beside himself. (Pardon the pun!)

3. Why do you think Adam was so enthusiastic about a woman he didn't know?

   _____

   _____

   _____

This passage illustrates a cornerstone principle of marriage. Just like Adam, you must individually receive your mate as God's provision for your need for companionship. Receiving your mate demonstrates your faith in God's integrity.

Adam's focus was on God's flawless character, not on Eve's performance. He knew God and he knew that God could be trusted. Adam enthusiastically received Eve because He knew she was from God. Adam's faith in God enabled him to receive Eve as God's perfect provision for him.

4. Complete the following sentence: If my fiancé(e) is God's provision for me, then receiving him or her as God's gift means that I should...

    _____

    _____

    _____

    _____

5. Consider the results of *not* receiving your mate. Describe what would happen to such a marriage in 10 or 20 years.

    _____

    _____

    _____

    _____

Before your marriage, you must receive your mate in the same way Adam received Eve. If you decide your fiancé(e) is indeed God's provision, you need to accept your fiancé(e)'s strengths *and* weaknesses. Will you unconditionally accept good habits (that are known) and bad habits (that you haven't learned yet)? Will you look beyond physical attractiveness to the God who is the provider, who knows what He is doing?

In addition, receiving your mate is not just a decision you make when reciting your wedding vows. It requires an attitude of *continual acceptance* throughout your marriage.

In the months and years after the wedding, each of you will become more and more aware of your respective weaknesses and faults. The more you remember your responsibility to receive each other as God's provision, the stronger your marriage will become. If the person who knows you best also loves you the most, your marriage will truly be special.

Commitment Number Two: Leave Your Parents

Let's read on in the Genesis account to uncover more of God's blueprints for marriage:

> "For this cause a man shall leave his father and his mother, and shall cleave to his wife; and they shall become one flesh" (Genesis 2:24).

As children, we are dependent upon our parents for the material and nonmaterial things in our lives. Our parents have the responsibility of providing food, shelter and clothing, as well as emotional stability, godly values and spiritual growth. But just as the doctor cuts the umbilical cord from the baby to the mother, so you must cut the umbilical cord of *dependency* and *allegiance* to your parents. If you don't, you'll undermine the interdependence you are to build as husband and wife.

Leaving involves two kinds of surgery:

- ♥ Severing the cord of dependency: This means choosing not to rely on your parents for material or emotional support. The wedding day is to a man or woman what the Fourth of July is to Americans—a declaration of independence.
- ♥ Severing the cord of allegiance: Before the wedding day, your most significant relationships are with your mother and father, but during that ceremony your priorities change. You should continue to honor your parents (see Exodus 20:12), but your priority must now become your spouse. Your first and foremost loyalty is to your spouse.

Both you and your parents must recognize this shift in loyalty and dependence. This act of breaking away from one's parents is absolutely foundational to establishing oneness.

6. In your own words, write a one sentence definition of what "a man shall leave his father and mother" means.

_____

_____

_____

_____

7. What are some common ways that individuals fail to cut the cord of *dependence* after they are married?

_____

_____

_____

_____

8. What are some common ways individuals fail to cut the cord of *allegiance*?

_____

_____

_____

_____

9. How would it make you feel if your spouse failed to sever the cord of dependency?

_____

_____

_____

_____

The cord of allegiance?

_____

_____

_____

10. Can you think of any areas that your parents, or your fiancé(e)'s parents, will find it difficult to let you leave?

_____

_____

_____

_____

Commitment Number Three: Cleave to Your Mate

To "cleave" (see Genesis 2:24) means to stick like glue. It is a permanent bond, not meant to be broken.

11. In a marriage relationship, the glue that keeps you together is (choose one):

❑ Expectations of extended family that I will never get a divorce because it would mar the family name

❑ The IRS exemptions

❑ The need to keep a divorce from impeding my career track

❑ A vow/covenant—a commitment of my will to honor my word, my spouse, and my God

❑ Guiltless sex

❑ Good communication and problem-solving skills

On your wedding day you will participate with your spouse in one of the most solemn responsibilities ever given to humankind—the vow of marriage. This vow, or covenant, is a life-long commitment, a promise not just between two people, but between a man and a woman and their God. Your marriage covenant involves three promises:

- To stay married throughout your lives;
- To love and care for each other;
- To maintain sexual fidelity.

One reason so many people divorce today is that they fail to enter into marriage with a firm commitment to fulfill their marriage covenant. Secretly, they think they can try someone else if this relationship doesn't work out.

It is your covenant—your sacred unconditional commitment made in the presence of Almighty God—that will create a secure marriage relationship. A partial commitment will only create fear and guarantee the failure of your marriage.

12. Read the following Scripture passages:

> "Take heed then, to your spirit, and let no one deal treacherously against the wife of your youth. For I hate divorce," says the LORD (Malachi 2:15,16).

> And some Pharisees came to [Jesus], testing Him, and saying, "Is it lawful for a man to divorce his wife for any cause at all?"

> And He answered and said, "Have you not read, that He who created them from the beginning made them male and female, and said, 'For this cause a man shall leave his father and mother, and shall cleave to his wife; and the two shall become one flesh'? Consequently they are no longer two, but one flesh. What therefore God has joined together, let no man separate" (Matthew 19:3-6).

Why do you think God feels so strongly about divorce? Think back on all you've learned so far about God's purposes and plans for marriage.

_____

_____

_____

_____

_____

_____

Author Elisabeth Elliot has said, "Love is to will another person's good." It is not based on feelings or emotions. This idea is at the heart of commitment. Commitment is willing another person's good through an unbreakable pledge of fidelity and devotion. It is an

unconditional, irrevocable promise to always be there. It is the res-
olute conviction of your will to stick to that person for life.

When two people display that type of commitment in marriage,
they truly fulfill God's purposes, and they become a witness to the
world of God's character. Divorce not only causes terrible damage to
you and to those you love, but it also brings shame upon the name
of Christ.

Commitment Number Four: Become One Flesh

The phrase "one flesh" (see Genesis 2:24) is the origin of the term
"oneness." That is why we say that, in marriage, one plus one equals
one!

Sexual intercourse is an integral part of becoming one flesh, but
not the whole. It involves deep relational intimacy. Here's what Dr.
Louis H. Evans, Jr. wrote about the term "one flesh":

> The one flesh in marriage is not just a physical phenom-
> enon, but a uniting of the totality of two personalities. In
> marriage, we are one flesh spiritually by vow, economical-
> ly by sharing, logistically by adjusting time and agreeing
> on the disbursement of all life's resources, experientially
> by trudging through the dark valleys and standing victo-
> riously on the peaks of success, and sexually by the bond-
> ing of our bodies.[1]

When you look at the place of becoming one flesh in God's plan for
marriage, it is clear that it should *follow* commitment—not precede
it. It's receive, leave, cleave and *then* become one flesh.

13. In other Scripture verses (see Mark 7:21, Romans 13:13,
    1 Thessalonians 4:3), God forbids sexual relations before mar-
    riage. Considering what we've learned up to now, answer the
    following objections to this commandment:

"We love each other—and we're going to be married anyway."

_____

_____

_____

"When we're together, it just feels so right. How could something so wonderful be wrong?"

_____

_____

_____

It's important to remember that God always has our best interest in mind. He designed sexual intercourse to strengthen a bond that He has already made strong—like placing steel reinforcing rods in concrete.

We'll get into far more detail about one flesh in Session Six, but notice the progression that God has established (see Genesis 2:18-25) as His blueprints for building a relationship:

* Man is alone.
* God recognizes his need.
* God provides for this need.
* Man receives that provision.
* Both leave father and mother.
* They cleave to one another.
* They become one flesh.
* They experience intimacy and oneness.

As you and your spouse daily embrace God's purposes (Session One) and His plan (Session Two) for marriage, you will begin the process of becoming one. Something is born on every wedding day. Before the wedding ceremony, there is *he* and *she*. After the ceremony there is a new entity called "us." This is the one flesh God speaks of—a growing, thriving, living relationship.

When you and your fiancé(e) are both committed to receiving, leaving, cleaving and becoming one flesh, you are building from

God's blueprints. Get ready for the divine mathematical mystery where one plus one equals one!

A Oneness Marriage

When you build a marriage according to God's blueprints, you experience the benefits of living according to His plan. Ecclesiastes 4:9,10 tell us: "Two are better than one because they have a good return for their labor. For if either of them falls, the one will lift up his companion. But woe to the one who falls when there is not another to lift him up."

A "oneness marriage" is the opposite of the world's 50/50 plan. It is a 100/100 plan in which both husband and wife set aside their own selfishness and experience true intimacy.

In our discussion about God's purposes and plans for marriage in these first two sessions, we've discussed the commitments that you need to build a solid marriage. Everything we've learned points to one central fact: For your marriage to become what God intended it to be, you must make a commitment to put God at the center of your relationship. The heart of a Oneness Marriage is an intensely spiritual relationship between one man and one woman and their God. It demands a lifelong process of relying on God and forging an enduring relationship according to His design.

In the final sessions of this workbook, we will provide practical advice on how to forge this type of marriage relationship. But before moving on, you would be wise to take time to evaluate the role of God in your relationship.

We'd like to challenge you with two questions that may be the most important you've ever considered:

IS CHRIST AT THE CENTER OF YOUR LIFE?

Many couples lose weight and get in the very best physical condition prior to their wedding day. They want to look and be their best for the honeymoon. Spiritually speaking, take a look in the mirror and analyze what you see.

- ♥ Have you ever received Christ as your Savior and Lord?
- ♥ Has God been at work in your life over the past couple of years?
- ♥ Are you growing in your relationship with Him?

If you have trouble answering any of these questions, we suggest reading the two appendixes to this workbook, "The Four Spiritual Laws" and "Have You Made the Wonderful Discovery of the Spirit-Filled Life?" From these resources you will learn more about how to experience a relationship with Christ.

IS GOD CALLING YOU TOGETHER AS MAN AND WIFE?

This is the critical question for any Christian couple contemplating marriage. To answer it requires:

♥ A biblical understanding of how God leads in our lives.
♥ A willingness to take an honest look at your relationship—your compatability, your strengths and weaknesses and your current ability to make a strong decision.

Following this session are two special projects that will guide you through the process of making a wise decision concerning marriage—"Evaluating Your Relationship" and "A Decision-Making Guide." If you are still deciding whether or not to get married, these projects will help you take a new look at your relationship and determine how God is leading you. If you are already engaged, they will help confirm your decision.

These projects are an integral part of this study and should be completed as soon as possible. Confirming your decision will aid you in dealing with doubts and will create security that your relationship needs to grow.

Navigating by true North:

Truths to chart your course

- The commitment to *receive* your mate as God's perfect provision for you must be based on faith in a God who can be trusted.
- The commitment to leave your parents means cutting the cords of dependence and allegiance.
- The commitment to cleave to your mate is an unconditional, irrevocable choice of your will. Marriage is a permanent, sacred covenant and not to be taken lightly.
- The commitment to become one flesh creates a divinely mysterious union—emotional, physical and spiritual transparency—that in God's plan must never precede marriage.
- When you build from God's blueprints, *one plus one equals one*.
- Marriage is an intensely spiritual relationship. Therefore, God must be at the center of your lives and of your marriage.

Couple's Project

Get Real

Interact as a couple on the following activities:

1. Spend a few minutes sharing and discussing your answers to the questions in "Get the Picture" and "Get the Truth." Be sure to ask your fiancé(e) to explain his or her answers.

2. Answer the following two questions individually, and then share your answers with each other:

   a. As you consider leaving your parents, which of the two cords—the cord of dependence or the cord of allegiance—will be the most difficult one for you to sever and why?

   _____

   _____

   _____

   b. Which of the two cords mentioned above will be most difficult for your fiancé(e) to sever? Why?

   _____

   _____

   _____

   _____

3. Discuss with your fiancé(e) ways in which you can honor each set of parents as you clearly cut the cords of dependency and allegiance.

    _____

    _____

    _____

    _____

4. What have been your feelings about divorce up to this point? How have those feelings been influenced by your own family history?

    _____

    _____

    _____

    _____

5. Indicate whether you agree or disagree with the following statement and tell why: "Jesus Christ is at the center of my life."

    _____

    _____

    _____

    _____

6. Indicate whether you agree or disagree with the following statement, and why: "Our relationship has a solid foundation with Christ at the center."

    _____

    _____

    _____

    _____

7. Conclude this section by writing a brief paragraph describing the position you want God to hold in your marriage:

_____

_____

_____

_____

_____

get to the Heart of your marriage—prayer

One of the best ways to learn to pray more effectively is to write out your prayers. Take a few moments and write down a two- or three-sentence prayer expressing your desire to build your marriage according to God's plan.

The following is a suggestion to help you get started:

> Dear God,
> It is our desire to build a marriage that honors You, the creator of marriage. To do that we both need to build according to Your plan. Today, we pledge to You that Your plan of receiving, leaving, cleaving and becoming one flesh will be the blueprint for our marriage. In Christ's name, amen.

After you have both jotted down a short prayer, kneel side by side, if you are able to, and together pray to God.

> Before the next session, complete the Life Map section in the Personal History Worksheet (if you haven't already done so) to prepare for the Session Three Couple's Project.

get Deeper

Here are two optional assignments for those who want to go deeper.

1. Read chapter 12 in *Staying Close* by Dennis Rainey.
2. For further information on honoring your parents, read *The Tribute and The Promise* by Dennis Rainey with Dave Boehi.

questions for those who were previously married

1. Did you find it difficult to receive your mate in your first marriage? In what ways?

    _____

    _____

    _____

    _____

2. Did you find it difficult to leave your parents? Why?

    _____

    _____

    _____

    _____

3. Did you begin the marriage with a commitment to stay married for life? As you look back now, what eroded that commitment?

    _____

    _____

    _____

    _____

4. What unique challenges will you face in each of the following
    areas in a new marriage?
    Receive:

    _____

    _____

    _____

    Leave:

    _____

    _____

    _____

    Cleave:

    _____

    _____

    _____

    Become one flesh:

    _____

    _____

    _____

5. If your fiancé(e) has children, how does this affect your ability
    to receive him or her as God's gift to you?

    _____

    _____

    _____

    _____

    _____

What kind of role do you expect to have in your future stepchildren's lives?

_____

_____

_____

_____

6. If you have children, what kind of role do you expect your future spouse to have in your children's lives?

_____

_____

_____

_____

How will you relate to your previous in-laws?

_____

_____

_____

_____

What kind of relationship will your children have with them?

_____

_____

_____

_____

1. Louis H. Evans, Jr., *Hebrews: The Communicator's Commentary Series* (Waco, Tex.: Word Publishing, 1985), p. 243.

evaLuatinG
your
ReLationship

No other human relationship will play a more important role in shaping your life than your relationship with your mate. And yet many people make the crucial decisions about marriage when their minds are clouded by such powerful emotions that they find it diffi-cult to think straight. They are so caught up in a whirlwind of emo-tions that they fail to work out some crucial issues before they com-mit their lives to each other.

This special project is designed to help you evaluate your rela-tionship and face some of these critical issues. Whether you and your partner are already engaged or just seriously contemplating marriage, working through this material will force you to ask some challenging questions about your relationship. Specifically, we want to help you...

* Eliminate any encumbrance that hinders you from think-ing clearly about the relationship;
* Evaluate your compatibility.

Yes, this process may seem unromantic. But if your goal is to build a true oneness marriage—an intimate relationship that is all God intended—then this decision needs to be made with your mind and will as well as your emotions.

If you have already decided to marry, then allow this section to confirm your direction. Stay open to what God wants for you. Ask the difficult questions. Have the courage to be honest.

If you have not yet decided, then allow this material to help guide you. As you work through this process, you can be confident that your decision is informed, balanced and biblical.

A Special Note

As we look at different aspects of evaluating your relationship, you may be challenged to look at yourself and your fiancé(e) in new ways. Don't feel pressured to come to make a decision about your future when you complete this section. In fact, we've placed it toward the beginning of this workbook so you can use it as a framework for making your decision.

SPIRITUAL COMPATIBILITY

Since marriage is a spiritual relationship, your spiritual compatibility will influence the quality of your relationship more than any other factor. There are two topics to consider here:

ARE BOTH OF YOU CHRISTIANS?
In 2 Corinthians 6:14,15, Paul writes:

> Do not be bound together with unbelievers; for what partnership have righteousness and lawlessness, or what fellowship has light with darkness? Or what harmony has Christ with Belial [Satan], or what has a believer in common with an unbeliever?

This passage warns that a Christian should not enter a partnership with an unbeliever because it will be a relationship built on opposing values and goals. Building relationships on Christian values, trust and love is essential to the Christian life, especially in the most intimate of all human relationships—marriage. God created marriage and its greatest fulfillment and enjoyment can only be found when both have a growing relationship with Him.

When Christians marry nonbelievers, they experience a growing frustration after marriage:

- They are unable to discuss the most precious, intimate part of their lives with their mates.
- They have conflicting goals and expectations.
- They clash over the values they teach their children.
- The have differing circles of friends.
- They have difficulty communicating and resolving conflict.

If one of you has received Christ, but the other has not, we strongly recommend that you either put your relationship on hold or end it altogether. Don't allow yourself to adopt a missionary mindset, where you think you can lead your partner to Christ, either before or after marriage. Bible teacher Dr. Howard Hendricks has a favorite statement: "As now, so then." If your partner is unwilling to repent and change now, don't expect it to happen after you marry.

Second, if neither of you has received Christ, we recommend that you put off any wedding plans so you can focus on learning more about a relationship with Him. Give yourselves time to talk with Christian friends or your pastor, and come to a solid decision about where you stand with God.

DO YOU BOTH SHARE THE SAME COMMITMENT TO SPIRITUAL GROWTH AND TO SERVING GOD?

Many Christians know they should not marry a nonbeliever. Unfortunately, they go no further in evaluating their spiritual compatibility.

First John 2:15 tells us, "Do not love the world, nor the things in the world. If anyone loves the world, the love of the Father is not in him." You may both have received Christ, but if one of you is more focused on loving the world than loving God, you will experience many of the same conflicts as a believer and nonbeliever. Your goals and values will differ. Your lives will head in different directions.

If you are both growing in Christ, however, you will experience a special joy and teamwork in your marriage. Running coaches usually encourage their long-distance runners to train in groups rather than alone. In a group, runners encourage and push each other to ignore their weariness and pain. In fact, a runner may run faster in a group than he would by himself, yet feel less fatigued. In the same way, two people who share the same commitment to God can encourage and help each other to keep their eyes on Christ as they "run with endurance the race that is set before" them (Hebrews 12:1).

To evaluate this area of your spiritual compatibility, begin by asking yourself questions such as:

- Do both of us share the same desire to know and please God?
- Do I have any sense that either one of us is putting on a facade of spiritual commitment?
- Do our actions back up our words?
- Do we both consistently display a desire to obey God in all things?
- What priority does each of us place on ministering to other people?
- Are we both willing to follow God's direction?

If you cannot shake a suspicion that you and your partner are on different wavelengths in your spiritual compatability, we strongly advise you to postpone any wedding plans. If not, you will likely experience a distressing level of isolation in your marriage.

1. How would you describe your spiritual compatibility at this time?

   _____

   _____

   _____

   _____

2. What changes would need to occur in *you* to increase your spiritual compatibility?

    _____

    _____

    _____

    _____

3. What changes would need to occur in *your fiancé(e)* to increase your spiritual compatibility?

    _____

    _____

    _____

    _____

Relational Compatibility

Building on the foundation of spiritual compatibility, you also need to evaluate the harmony of your everyday relationship. This means examining your relational skills, the quality of your friendship and the way your two personalities mesh.

If you are meeting with a premarital counselor, you may already have completed some type of personality or temperament survey. Tests such as the Taylor-Johnson Temperament Analysis, the PRE-PARE test, the DiSC test or the Myers-Briggs Type Indicator will give you invaluable information to see how well you and your partner mesh. If you are not planning to complete one of these tests, this exercise will help provide a basic understanding of how well you fit together.

1. Complete the chart below. Put an X on the number that best describes you on each quality or trait. Put a circle around the number that best describes your partner.

Disciplined	1	2	3	4	5	6	7	8	9	10	Impulsive
Stubborn	1	2	3	4	5	6	7	8	9	10	Humble
Aggressive/											Compliant/
assertive	1	2	3	4	5	6	7	8	9	10	passive
Task-oriented	1	2	3	4	5	6	7	8	9	10	People-oriented
Pessimistic	1	2	3	4	5	6	7	8	9	10	Optimistic
Fast-paced	1	2	3	4	5	6	7	8	9	10	Slow-paced
Socially active	1	2	3	4	5	6	7	8	9	10	Withdrawn
Sympathetic	1	2	3	4	5	6	7	8	9	10	Insensitive
Decisive	1	2	3	4	5	6	7	8	9	10	Indecisive
Tense	1	2	3	4	5	6	7	8	9	10	Relaxed
Emotionally											Emotionally
open	1	2	3	4	5	6	7	8	9	10	closed
Good self-image	1	2	3	4	5	6	7	8	9	10	Poor self-image
Critical	1	2	3	4	5	6	7	8	9	10	Patient
Idealistic	1	2	3	4	5	6	7	8	9	10	Realistic
Controlling	1	2	3	4	5	6	7	8	9	10	Permissive
Affectionate	1	2	3	4	5	6	7	8	9	10	Reserved
Verbal	1	2	3	4	5	6	7	8	9	10	Quiet
Responsible	1	2	3	4	5	6	7	8	9	10	Irresponsible

2. In what areas do you and your partner balance each other?

_____

_____

_____

_____

3. How have you seen your differences benefit your relationship?

_____

_____

_____

4. What differences have caused friction and conflict in your relationship?

_____

_____

_____

_____

5. Does anything here cause you to doubt whether you should continue the relationship?

_____

_____

_____

_____

A Word About Compatibility and Commitment

There is no black-and-white formula for evaluating all these factors. The key is how they play out in your relationship and how you feel about them. For example, you may be concerned that your hobbies and recreational interests are quite different. Yet you may find that the few things that you do enjoy doing together outweigh those differences.

It's also interesting to note that God often seems to bring together two people who are different in many ways. For example, a fast-paced wife ends up marrying a slower-paced husband. A people-oriented husband chooses a task-oriented mate.

So identifying your similarities and differences in these areas is only the first step toward determining compatibility. You also need to address two other areas:

- ♥ How your differences may make you stronger as a team;
- ♥ How your commitment could compensate for your differences.

Relational Fog Producers

When air temperature, ground temperature, humidity and barometric pressure come together in just the right combination, clouds that once floated 5,000 feet overhead hug the ground. When fog rolls into a city, the airport shuts down, traffic is snarled and the engines of progress sputter.

Have you ever tried to drive in a dense fog? It's an eerie feeling. All you can see is the area directly in front of you. Buildings and other vehicles seem like ghosts. Sounds are muted.

It's also dangerous, especially if you proceed too fast. And yet many couples can be compared to a driver speeding at 60 miles per hour through a dense fog, supremely confident that they'll make it through yet having no idea what lies 30 feet ahead. Where once they saw clearly, now their minds are clouded by conflicting emotions, yet they press on in the relationship without slowing down.

The list of fog producers in a serious relationship could be endless. In our experience, we have identified eight that are most common and most serious.

IDEALISTIC THINKING

In the excitement of this relationship, everything seems wonderful. You have a difficult time discerning any faults in this person who is all you ever dreamed of. Another word for this state of mind could be "infatuation."

LONELINESS

You're tired of living on your own and you long for the companionship of marriage. You feel the pressure of well-meaning family and friends who ask, "Do you have anyone in your life?" You wonder if something is wrong with you. You aren't getting any younger, and if you're a woman, you probably feel the inevitable ticking of your biological clock.

WEDDING PREPARATIONS

Planning a wedding is like riding a runaway train. The faster you go, the harder it is to stop. Even if you have some serious doubts, the thought of canceling or postponing a wedding is unbearable. What would people think?

SEXUAL INVOLVEMENT

You have had or are engaging in sexual intercourse, heavy petting, or excessive kissing and touching. Premarital sexual involvement leads to an emotional bonding that prevents you from clearly evaluating other aspects of the relationship. It also can produce guilt or shame that lingers on into marriage.

SPIRITUAL IMMATURITY

One or both of you may be in a period of rebellion, walking out of fellowship with God. This may be the temporary result of unconfessed sin in your life, or it may be a long-term pattern going back many years. Or you may sincerely desire to grow in your relationship with Christ, but you don't know how. You have no sense of how God may be leading in the relationship because you have no idea how to discern His voice.

Special Note

The first five fog producers may lead you to make an unwise or premature commitment to your fiancé(e). The final three, however, may *prevent* you from making a commitment.

FEAR OF FAILURE

You are troubled by thoughts of not living up to the expectations of your fiancé(e), your peers, your family or yourself. You feel you will be unable to make a marriage work. Perhaps your parents' marriage ended in divorce and you don't want that to happen to you.

FEAR OF COMMITMENT

While you long for the benefits of marriage, you feel a deep, profound, grave sense of dread when you contemplate making a lifelong commitment to another person. You realize that if someone better comes along, you are stuck. You are paralyzed from moving ahead.

THE INABILITY OR UNWILLINGNESS TO SEEK AND GIVE FORGIVENESS

When your fiancé(e) has hurt you, he or she is unable or unwilling to admit the offense and seek your forgiveness. Or when you have hurt him or her, he or she is unable or unwilling to forgive you.

1. Look over this list of seven relational fog producers. Which of them *are* issues in your relationship?

   _____

   _____

   _____

   _____

2. If you have some serious concerns, are you willing to take the time you need to ensure you make a good decision about marriage? Why or why not?

   _____

   _____

   _____

   _____

If you have some concerns, talk with a counselor, pastor or mentor about them.

Heeding Relational Red flags

Any relationship will have its difficulties, but sometimes those difficulties are indicators of deep-rooted problems that, if not addressed quickly, will poison your marriage. If any of the following caution signs exist in your relationship, we recommend you talk about the situation as soon as possible with a pastor, counselor or mentor.

RED FLAGS OF RELATIONAL DIFFICULTIES[1]
1. You have a general uneasy feeling that there is something wrong in your relationship with your fiancé(e).
2. You find yourself arguing often with your fiancé(e).
3. Your fiancé(e) seems irrationally jealous whenever you interact with someone of the opposite sex.

4. You avoid discussing certain subjects because you're afraid of your fiancé(e)'s reaction.

5. Your fiancé(e) finds it extremely difficult to express emotions, or is prone to extreme emotions (such as out-of-control anger or exaggerated fear) or swinging back and forth between emotional extremes (such as being very happy one minute, then suddenly exhibiting extreme sadness the next).

6. Your fiancé(e) displays controlling behavior. This means more than wanting to be in charge—it means your fiancé(e) seems to want to control every aspect of your life: your appearance, your lifestyle, your interactions with friends or family, etc. Your fiancé(e) seems to manipulate you into doing what he or she wants.

7. You are continuing the relationship because of fear—fear of hurting your fiancé(e) or fear of what he or she might do if you ended the relationship.

8. Your fiancé(e) does not treat you with respect. He or she constantly criticizes you or talks sarcastically to you.

9. Your fiancé(e) is unable to hold down a job, doesn't take personal responsibility for losing a job, or he or she frequently borrows money from you or friends.

10. Your fiancé(e) often talks about imagined aches and pains, going from doctor to doctor until he or she finds someone who will agree that he or she is seriously ill.

11. Your fiancé(e) is unable to resolve conflict. He or she cannot deal with constructive criticism, never admits a mistake and never asks for forgiveness.

12. Your fiancé(e) is overly-dependent on parents for finances, decision-making or emotional security.

13. Your fiancé(e) shows a pattern of dishonesty, rationalizing questionable behavior or twisting words to his or her benefit.

14. Your fiancé(e) exhibits patterns of physical, emotional or sexual abuse toward you or others. If he or she has ever threatened to hit you or actually struck you, this is a warning sign of future abuse. If he or she puts you down or continually criticizes you, this is a sign of emotional abusiveness.

15. Your fiancé(e) displays signs of drug or alcohol abuse: unexplained absences or missed dates, frequent car accidents, the smell of alcohol or strong odor of mouthwash, erratic behavior

or emotional swings, physical signs such as red eyes, unkempt look, unexplained nervousness etc.

16. Your fiancé(e) displayed a sudden, dramatic change in lifestyle as you began dating. (He or she may be changing just to win you and will revert back to old habits after marriage.)

Do you recognize any of these caution signs in your relationship? If so, which ones?

_____

_____

_____

_____

If so, we recommend you talk about the situation as soon as possible with a pastor, counselor or mentor.

Special Warning

If any of these caution signs are present in your relationship *and* you are engaging in sexual intercourse, it is imperative that you terminate the physical intimacy immediately. As we've already discussed, God has your welfare in mind when He forbids sexual connection before marriage. The premature bond this type of intimacy creates will make it extremely difficult for you to make needed changes in your relationship or to break it off.

1. Adapted by permission from Bob Phillips, *How Can I Be Sure: A Pre-Marriage Inventory* (Eugene, Ore.; Harvest House Publishers Inc., 1978).

a Decision-making Guide:
Helping you move from "Do I?" to "I do!" or "I don't"

It's as inevitable as night following day: As their relationship grows more serious, two people begin asking the question, "Is God leading us to marry?" It's a key question because receiving each other as God's provision requires a conviction that He has brought you together.

Many Christians find it difficult to explain how they determine God's will for important decisions in their lives. Ask 100 Christians,

"How do you know God's will?" and you will receive so many different answers that you will wonder if they read the same Bible.

We asked a number of married couples, "How did you determine
whether God was calling you to be married?" Here are some of their
answers:

> "From the moment I saw her I knew she was special. We
> used to look into each other's eyes and ask each other if
> we were really supposed to be together and we literally
> would get this real tingly feeling, both of us together at
> the same time. It's hard to explain. It gave chills through
> my whole body."

> "I knew she would be good for me. Her personality really
> complements mine. The things that I am weak in she is
> strong in. She is a godly woman and I just felt like she was
> the one for me, I guess. I can't point to anything concrete
> besides the fact that we spent time praying about it, but
> at a certain point the timing was just right and we were
> just relying on God's timing. And I felt like I didn't have
> a red light from God. He didn't stop me."

> "We hit it off as such close friends. I felt like I had known
> her for my whole life. Also, she was a Christian. At that
> time, I thought I was a Christian and I wanted to marry
> someone that I knew believed as I did. So I knew it was
> God's will."

As you can see, Christians have many different ideas about how
to know God's will. The problem is that sometimes we receive mis-
information, especially on the subject of choosing a mate. For example, many Christians believe they will have a feeling of peace if they
are following God's will. Yet, sometimes, following God's leading
may lead to great fear and anxiety, like going to someone you've hurt
to apologize and seek forgiveness. Our feelings and emotions are so
fickle that to depend on them as an indicator of God's will is like
deciding to go to work each day based on the weather.

Another common belief is, "God will do something to keep me from making a mistake in choosing a marriage partner." The reality, however, is that they may be looking for His voice in the wrong places. They may not be accustomed to listening to His Spirit within their hearts.

On the other end of the spectrum is the belief that, apart from what God specifically states in Scripture to do or not to do, we are on our own. Therefore, it doesn't matter whom you marry, as long as the two of you are compatible and you're not disobeying Scripture. However, this philosophy often limits the ministry of the Holy Spirit. The Spirit not only speaks to us through the Word of God but also influences us through other means (though never in contradiction with the Word). The Bible clearly states that God leads in the lives of individuals; the Holy Spirit not only teaches, but guides.

Going through this decision making process is one of the most important steps you can take to ensure a oneness marriage:

1. It will help you determine how God is leading in your relationship.
2. It will formally seal the decision you have made to marry.
3. It will give you a landmark to look back on during times of doubt and fear.
4. It will provide a milestone for you 5, 10, 20 years into your marriage that you can look back on and see how God was leading in your lives.
5. It is a healthy process for a couple to work through regardless of whether you are engaged or not because it will ground you in the Word of God and encourage you to keep growing in your relationship with Him.

As in the previous special project, we suggest you complete the following material individually and then discuss it together.

Special Note

If you are deciding whether to become engaged, this project will help you learn how to discern God's will. As you read through it, do not feel pressured to make the decision now. This guide provides you with a biblical framework for making the decision—when you believe it is time to make it.

If you already are engaged, this guide will help you think through some critical issues to ensure you did not overlook anything regarding your decision. You may find your decision confirmed or challenged in some areas. Of all the decisions you will make in life, this is one that you will want to expose to the rigors of added scrutiny. Don't be afraid to test your decision by making this project a decision review.

COMPONENTS of a BIBLICAL DECISION

Picture the framework of a biblical decision as a wheel with four spokes. Each part of the wheel represents a necessary component in a biblical decision.

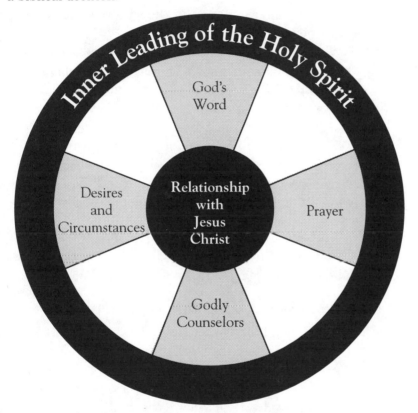

Hub of the Wheel: Your Relationship with Jesus Christ

It is in knowing Him, loving Him, obeying Him, talking with Him, seeking Him—in other words, *relating* to Him—that we come to know His will.

In the Gospel of John, Jesus describes Himself as a shepherd who cares for His sheep. "I am the good shepherd; and I know My own, and My own know Me. My sheep hear My voice, and I know them, and they follow Me" (John 10:14,27).

As you develop an intimate relationship with Christ you will come to know His voice—how He speaks to you, how He leads in your life. And the more you know God, the more you are willing to trust Him with your life.

First Spoke of the Wheel: God's Word

By spending time reading the Bible you allow God to speak to you directly. In some cases, God's Word will address areas of your relationship that are not pleasing to Him. It will also provide wisdom and guidance as you make your decision.

Psalm 119:105 states, "Thy word is a lamp to my feet, and a light to my path." As we've seen, God's Word provides guidelines for a marriage relationship. Secondly, Psalm 66:18 warns us that if we let sin control us, we will not hear the voice of God.

Second Spoke: Prayer

James 1:5 says, "But if any of you lacks wisdom, let him ask of God, who gives to all men generously and without reproach, and it will be given to him." We need to ask God for wisdom. In other words, we need to pray.

These first two spokes—God's Word and prayer—are the primary ways that the Holy Spirit directs your decision. Through asking (prayer) and seeking (time in God's Word) the Holy Spirit guides.

Third Spoke: Godly Counselors

As Proverbs 19:20 says, "Listen to counsel and accept discipline, that you may be wise the rest of your days." By consulting with mature, godly friends or family members—or with a Christian premarriage counselor—you benefit from their experience and perspective. Someone who has traveled farther down the road you are walking can provide valuable insight.

Additionally, because they are not so close to the details and emotions, they can offer a big-picture perspective. They may be able to spot strengths and weaknesses in your relationship much quicker than you. They also may be able to help you sort through your emotions and make a clearer decision. It is important that you seek out a godly counselor who will tell you what you *need* to hear, not someone who tells you what you *want* to hear.

Fourth Spoke: Desires and Circumstances

Often, in our efforts to find God's will, we deny our own personal preferences and desires. Philippians 2:13 states, "for it is God who is at work in you, both to will and to work for His good pleasure." You see, God does place desires within us for our good. Assuming you are growing in your relationship with the Lord and seeking His will, recognizing your desires can be an important part of the process. For example, do you *want* to be married at this point in your life? Do you *want* to marry *this* particular person? Is there anything about this person that you particularly dislike or that makes you feel particularly uncomfortable?

In addition, as you look at your relationship, ask yourself whether events and circumstances seem to confirm that the relationship is heading in the right direction. Questions like these may have surfaced as you completed the "Evaluating Your Relationship" project.

Rim of the Wheel: Inner Leading of the Holy Spirit

As you spend time with God, read the Bible, pray, seek godly counsel, consider your compatibility, desires and circumstances, and whole-heartedly submit to God, the Holy Spirit will guide you. The Scriptures tell us the Holy Spirit guides (see John 16:13) and teaches us (see 14:26) and that He is our Helper (see 14:16,26). Parakletos (the Greek word often used in the New Testament to describe the Holy Spirit) means "one called to the side of another with a view to providing help."

God may not speak in an audible voice to Christians today, as He did in the Old Testament and as He did through His Son, Jesus Christ, but He still speaks to our hearts.

Many Christians, as they seek God's will, look for some sort of miraculous sign. They want God to speak to them as He did to Moses—through a burning bush or a billboard that says, "Marry her! This is My will for you!" Instead, God gave us His Spirit to live in us as a means of disclosing His will to us. We have moment-by-moment access to God's guidance and counsel. Our job is to stay close to God, to keep in step with the Spirit (see Galatians 5:25), to listen and obey and yield to His leading.

The Holy Spirit uses three primary means of conveying the will of God:

   1. He speaks through His Word, the Bible. You are reading

a passage of Scripture for perhaps the twentieth time, but this time it becomes clearer than ever before and you realize it applies to a problem you're facing. The Spirit serves as our Teacher as we pour through God's Word.

2. He reveals how God is working. In their outstanding study guide, *Experiencing God*, Henry T. Blackaby and Claude V. King explain that in Scripture, God's usual pattern is to reveal to individuals what He is doing, then invite them to join Him in this work. Sometimes this experience feels like scales falling from your eyes. You look at your circumstances or your relationship, and suddenly you see it in a different perspective. You look back over the months and suddenly see the hand of God bringing you together—or perhaps you realize that He has worked in your heart in such a way that you know this relationship is *not* His will. In whatever situation, you have a definite sense that God has worked in your life.

3. He speaks through the development of inner convictions. As you look at your circumstances, you see them in a new light that clarifies what you need to do. You are talking with a neighbor and suddenly you sense an unmistakable impression that you should tell her about what Christ means to you.

A conviction from the Holy Spirit grows and matures over time. As you spend time with God, in hours of prayer and Bible study, you know what God desires in your life. For example:

- A middle-aged executive is disillusioned and unfulfilled in his career and he has a growing desire to be directly involved in helping others know Christ. After a few months, he realizes God has given him the conviction to work in full-time Christian ministry.
- Both parents of three young children work and are able to afford a large, beautiful home as a result. Over time, however, they become concerned about the high number of hours they devote to their careers. They realize God has put it on their hearts to make their children a greater priority in their lives so they make three decisions: The

husband reduces the number of hours he works each week, the wife decides to do work part-time out of her home and they reduce their monthly house payment by moving into a smaller home.

In the same way, God can give you a conviction about whether He wants you to marry. However, the Holy Spirit's internal guidance must always be consistent with His own character and ministry. That means three things will always be true of His leading:

- It will glorify Christ.
- It will promote holiness.
- It will be consistent with God's Word.

How Does Your Wheel Look?

As you evaluate your own decision-making process for making your decision about whether to be married, what does your wheel look like? Do you have the right hub at the center? Are all the spokes connected to the hub and rim? Are any of the spokes missing or shorter than they need to be?

Beside each question below, answer yes, no, or put a ? if you are uncertain.

_____ Is Christ the center of your life?

_____ Are you growing in spiritual maturity?

_____ Are you consistently praying and spending time in God's Word?

_____ Have you opened your relationship to the scrutiny of godly counselors?

_____ Have you weighed your desires?

_____ Have you evaluated your circumstances?

Finally:

_____ As you look at all these factors, is the Holy Spirit leading you in a specific direction?

If you and your fiancé(e) can answer yes to all of these questions, you can be confident you are moving in the right direction. If you cannot answer yes to each question, you need to take the time to address each issue.

a DECISON-makING pROCess

Once you understand the framework of a biblical decision, it's time to work through a process to make your decision.

- Will I receive this person as God's provision for me?
- Do I choose to commit myself to this person's good for the rest of my life?

To work through the following process you'll need to set aside a few hours and find a secluded spot where you can be alone without distractions or interruptions.

Step One: Spend Time Alone with God

Begin by spending time praising God for who He is. You might want to take a book of Christian songs and hymns, or read through some Psalms. Force yourself to take your mind off everything else in your life. You may find that it takes one or two hours just to relax and focus on God.

Then, make sure you are in fellowship with God by acknowledging any unconfessed sin. As Psalm 66:18 says, "If I regard wickedness in my heart, the Lord will not hear."

Step Two: Declare Your Willingness to Follow God's Will, No Matter What It Is

Many Christians never sense God's will in their lives because they have not taken this crucial step. Follow the advice of the great saint George Mueller who wrote about the process he followed in determining God's will:

> I seek at the beginning to get my heart into such a state that it has no will of its own in regard to a given matter. Nine-tenths of the trouble with people generally is just here. Nine-tenths of the difficulties are overcome when our hearts are ready to do the Lord's will, whatever it may be. When one is truly in this state, it is usually but a little way to the knowledge of what His will is.

Step Three: Make an Honest Evaluation of Your Relationship

Perhaps the most common cause of divorce today is irreconcilable differences. Two people who entered marriage with stars in their eyes find that after a few years of trying, they just cannot get along anymore.

The tragedy is that many of these marriages would never have occurred if the couple had been honest about their relationship before they made such a binding commitment. Their emotions were so strong and their desire to marry so overpowering that they failed to look deeply at questions of character, personality and background.

Special Note

If you haven't already done so, be sure to complete and discuss "Special Project 3: Evaluating Your Relationship" with your fiancé(e) before continuing with this project. The evaluation gives you the opportunity to ask some tough questions about your respective levels of spiritual maturity and you'll look for possible areas of conflict in how you relate to each other. You will find a list of issues that could create a fog in your relationship, making it difficult to make a good decision. Finally, a list of potential red flags is included that could indicate a need to proceed with great caution.

If you have already completed and discussed Special Project 3 with your fiancé(e), it might be a good idea to revisit your answers before continuing with this decision-making guide.

If you have any strong concerns after completing Special Project 3, talk to your mentor couple/pastor/counselor about any issues that are a concern to you.

Step Four: Consider Whether This Person Is God's Provision for You

Start by writing down five reasons why you think this is the right person for you to marry. Consider your responses throughout this workbook, the feedback you've received from godly counselors and the impressions you've received from the Holy Spirit.

1. _____
2. _____
3. _____
4. _____
5. _____

Now write five reasons why you think this is the right *time* to marry.

1. _____
2. _____
3. _____
4. _____
5. _____

Next, write a one sentence statement why you believe you are ready to *receive* this person as God's provision for you.

_____

_____

_____

_____

If you are troubled by fears or doubts, write them down. Honestly evaluate each fear or doubt by asking yourself the following two questions:

- Is this doubt the result of legitimate questions in my mind?
- Does it demonstrate any lack of trust in God?

_____

_____

_____

Plan a time to talk these over with your fiancé(e). Keep the following questions in mind as you discuss your doubts.

- Did he or she receive or resist my concerns?
- Is he or she open to correcting these relationship problems?
- Is he or she willing and able to give and ask for forgiveness?

Step Five: Make a Decision and Act on It by Faith

Once you decide how God is leading in your relationship, your responsibility is to obey by faith.

If you decide to become engaged, move forward with confidence. If doubts arise, discuss them openly and honestly. Ask God to continue to confirm your decision over the weeks and months ahead.

If you decide not to get engaged, move forward with confidence. Though this choice entails incredible emotional heartache, you can act by faith, knowing you made the decision through a biblical framework.

- Ask God to help you end the relationship in a way that is honoring to Him. Show dignity, respect, kindness and honor toward the other person.
- Make a clean break. We strongly suggest that there be no communication for six months. It will be wise to make yourself accountable to someone who can give godly counsel to hold you to this commitment.
- After this time if you think God may be leading you back together, you should seek wise counsel before reestablishing contact.

Remember, God's will is not something that is lost so that you need to find it. It is not something that He is keeping from you, leaking out hints along the way or keeping you guessing so that you never quite know what to do.

On the contrary, God's will is clearly revealed in His Word. He has given you the Holy Spirit to guide you in His Word, and to give you understanding and insight. The most important thing you can do in determining God's will is to walk closely with Him, cultivating and developing your relationship with Him moment by moment.

Part Three

BUILDING
ONENESS

*In an era of increasingly fragile marriages, a
couple's ability to communicate is the single
most important contributor to a stable
and satisfying marriage.*

—Gallup Poll Report

authentic communication: avoiding the post-wedding letdown

true north

THE EXTENT TO WHICH YOU CAN LISTEN TO UNDERSTAND YOUR SPOUSE, EXPRESS YOURSELF TO BE UNDERSTOOD AND ACTIVELY RESOLVE CONFLICT BETWEEN THE TWO OF YOU WILL GREATLY DETERMINE THE LEVEL OF INTIMACY AND ONENESS YOU WILL EXPERIENCE IN YOUR MARRIAGE.

It has been said that communication is to a relationship what blood is to the human body. Communication nourishes and sustains a relationship. Remove it and you no longer have a relationship.

Perhaps that is why, whenever FamilyLife surveys couples attending our FamilyLife Marriage Conferences, so many ask for help about communication and conflict:

- "How can I express my feelings without feeling selfish?"
- "I always seem to say the wrong thing to hurt my husband's feelings. What can I do to prevent this?"
- "How can we change the patterns of our marriage into a deeper level of intimacy?"
- "How can we communicate without putting each other on the defensive?"
- "Why do we argue so much?"
- "How can I overcome this inability to express my feelings to my spouse on a permanent and regular basis?"

No doubt, your communication as a couple may feel quite gratifying. Most couples in the process of premarital counseling find that one of the joys of their relationship is that they can, and do, talk about everything.

However, while your word count may be high, your level of *real communication* may actually be lower than you think. Authentic communication is much more than just talking. It is understanding and being understood; identifying a tone of voice; detecting nonverbal cues; responding appropriately to offense; resolving conflicts; knowing what to say, when to say it and how to say it; experiencing the risks and rewards of knowing and being known; and much more.

As you learned in the first two sessions, marriage is built upon a foundation of a relationship with God. As you establish this spiritual foundation as a couple, it is essential that you see the importance of communication in your relationship.

get the picture

Read the case study, then answer the questions that follow:

Case Study: Bob and Sherry's Communication Problems

"She makes me so mad I could scream."

Bob was enjoying a day of fishing with Lee, an older friend at work. Their relationship had developed to the point that Bob looked forward to the conversation as much as the fishing.

This morning, Bob was frustrated about the conflict he and Sherry had experienced the night before. It had started over something that seemed so insignificant—a comment he had made over dinner about their plans to spend Christmas with his family. Sherry had fallen silent, and he had learned that this meant she was upset about something. "What's wrong?" he asked.

"Nothing," she replied.

"Then why do you have that look on your face? That's how you act when you're angry with me about something."

"I don't want to talk about it now," Sherry said.

"Right, you never want to talk about it. Do you think that whatever is bothering you will just go away? Sherry, if there's a problem, we need to talk it out."

With that, Sherry went into the bedroom and locked the door.

"So there I was," Bob told Lee. "I pounded my fist on the door and said, 'We'll never get this resolved if you don't come out! You can't hide in there forever!' She just turned on the television and never left the room the rest of the night. I slept on the couch."

Lee cast a lure to a partially submerged log, hoping to coax a largemouth bass out of hiding. Then he turned to Bob. "Something tells me that you and Sherry go through this same pattern every time you have a problem," he said. "You want to get in there and work out the conflict, and she wants to run and hide."

"Right, she never wants to talk," Bob said.

"Okay," Lee said, "let me ask you this: How is your communication at other times? Do you spend much time talking to each other?"

"About what?"

Lee smiled and said, "I think I just uncovered part of your problem."

1. Why do you think many couples experience so little conflict during courtship and engagement?

_____

_____

_____

_____

_____

2. If you were Lee, what would you do to help Bob learn how to communicate with Sherry?

_____

_____

_____

_____

_____

 # ǥet tHe tRutH

Any engaged couple will argue or disagree about things. But often they are so caught up in the whirlwind of romance and wedding plans that they really don't experience much conflict. So they're surprised when the storm inevitably sweeps into their home.

While conflict is inevitable, one of the greatest values of courtship and engagement is the opportunity to develop your ability to communicate effectively. To avoid the "Post-Wedding Letdown," we suggest learning a few basic communication skills.

Listening to Understand

The Bible has so much to say about the act of communicating because God knew it would not be a skill that comes easily for us. We've got to work at it. But in doing so, we grow in our dependence upon Him and in our relationship with others.

1. State in your own words the listening principle found in each of the following passages of Scripture.

    a. "But let everyone be quick to hear, slow to speak and slow to anger" (James 1:19).
    Listening Principle

    _____

    _____

    _____

    _____

    b. "A wise man will hear and increase in learning, a man of understanding will acquire wise counsel" (Proverbs 1:5)
    Listening Principle

    _____

    _____

    _____

    _____

2. What are some practical ways that you could apply these listening principles in your relationship right now?

    _____

    _____

    _____

    _____

Listening is hard work. It requires hearing with more than our ears—we use our eyes and our hearts as well. That is why authentic communication requires proper listening habits:

Proper Listening Habits

Focus on...	Rather than...
What is being said	How you feel about what is said
The way it is being said: tone of voice, posture, etc.	The words only
Clarification of valid points	Defense of incorrect accusations
Questions	Indictments
Understanding	Judgment

LISTENING QUESTIONS

Clarifying questions: "Are you telling me that _____?"

"What did you mean when you said _____?"

Summary questions: "Of all that you just said, what do you most want me to understand?"

"What do you need from me most right now?"

3. How do you think that adopting proper listening habits and using appropriate listening questions would help you in resolving a conflict?

_____

_____

_____

_____

_____

Expressing to Be Understood

4. State in your own words the listening principle found in each of the following Scriptures:

a. "Let no unwholesome word proceed from your mouth, but only such a word as is good for edification according to the need of the moment, that it may give grace to those who hear" (Ephesians 4:29).
Speaking Principle

_____

_____

_____

_____

b. "When there are many words, transgression is unavoidable, but he who restrains his lips is wise" (Proverbs 10:19).
Speaking Principle

_____

_____

_____

_____

c. "There is an appointed time for everything. And there is a time for every event under heaven—a time to be silent, and a time to speak" (Ecclesiastes 3:1,7).
Speaking Principle

_____

_____

_____

5. What are some practical ways that you could apply these principles in your relationship right now?

_____

_____

_____

_____

In the same way that we must actually seek clarification as a listener, we must also be deliberate with regard to what, how and when we choose to express ourselves. As a rule of thumb, consider the following steps toward expressing yourself:

Determining what you want to say:

+ What are my assumptions?
+ What are my beliefs?
+ What are my desires?
+ What are my dreams?
+ What are my needs?

Determine how you want to say it:

+ With excitement?
+ With sadness?
+ With conviction?
+ With disappointment?
+ With encouragement?

Determine when you want to say it:

+ During or after a meal?
+ During recreation?
+ At bedtime?
+ In the presence of childen?
+ While driving?

6. How do you think these speaking skills would help you in resolving a conflict?

_____

_____

_____

_____

The Scriptures have a lot to say about the power of the tongue—and of the listening ear. If you want to develop an intimate marriage relationship, you would be wise to speak less and listen more. The person who speaks less is more willing to set his or her own selfishness aside and build oneness in a marriage. He or she is better able to understand another viewpoint and is willing to seek the best for his or her mate.

Resolving Conflict

All of the communications skills discussed so far in this session will prove invaluable in helping you resolve a conflict in your relationship. But there are two more important principles for you to apply:

7. What does the following verse have to say about resolving conflict?

   "Be angry, and yet do not sin; do not let the sun go down on your anger" (Ephesians 4:26).

   Resolving conflict means…

   _____

   _____

   _____

   _____

8. What would happen in a relationship when this principle is not applied?

   _____

   _____

   _____

In marriage, it's common for both individuals to react to conflict in different ways. Here are four of the most common:

- **Fight to win:** This is the "I win, you lose" or "I'm right, you're wrong" position. You seek to dominate the other person; personal relationships take second place to the need to triumph.
- **Withdraw:** You seek to avoid discomfort at all costs, saying, "I'm uncomfortable, so I'll get out." You see no hope of resolving the conflict, or you lack the strength to confront it. So you cope by giving your mate the "silent treatment."

- ♥ **Yield:** You assume it is far better to go along with the other person's demands than risk a confrontation. "Rather than start another argument, whatever you wish is fine." To you, a safe feeling is more important than a close relationship.
- ♥ **Lovingly resolve:** You commit to resolving the conflict by taking steps to carefully and sensitively discuss the issue. Resolving a conflict requires a special attitude—one of humility, of placing the relationship at a higher priority than the conflict itself. You value your relationship more than winning or losing, escaping or feeling comfortable.

With three of these styles, you actually create as many problems as you solve. Fighting to win, withdrawing or yielding may allow you to escape, temporarily, from the conflict at hand, but you haven't really dealt with the emotions the conflict sparked—the hurt, the resentment and the anger. Only when you seek to confront each other in a loving way will you resolve a conflict.

9. What does the following verse have to say about resolving conflict?

    "And be kind to one another, tender-hearted, forgiving each other, just as God in Christ also has forgiven you" (Ephesians 4:32).
    Resolving conflict means…

    _____

    _____

    _____

    _____

10. What would happen in a relationship when this principle is not applied?

    _____

    _____

    _____

    _____

Resolving conflict also requires forgiveness—giving up the right to punish the one who has wronged you. This is the miracle of the Christian life: that we can heal our relationships with others in the same way Christ healed our relationship with Him through forgiveness.

NAVIGATING BY TRUE NORTH

TRUTHS TO CHART YOUR COURSE

- Authentic communication is much more than just talking. It requires understanding, being understood, identifying a tone of voice, detecting nonverbal clues, responding appropriately to offense, resolving conflicts, and knowing what to say, when to say it and how to say it. It is experiencing the risks and rewards of knowing and being known.
- Authentic communication means that the listener employs *clarifying* and *summary* questions.
- Resolving conflict requires a determination to lovingly confront each other.
- Resolving conflict requires forgiveness.

Couple's Project

get real

1. Spend a few minutes reading through "Get the Picture" and "Get the Truth," sharing and discussing your answers to the different questions. Be sure to ask your fiancé(e) to explain the answers.

2. When there is static on the phone line, little communication takes place. What you say and what you hear is fuzzy, unclear and often unintelligible. In your everyday communication with your fiancé(e), you'll find static of another kind. It has nothing to do with electricity, but it will short circuit your communication just the same. If you fail to anticipate this interference and make the necessary adjustments, you will experience difficulty communicating.

   Each individual has a basic pattern of expressiveness. One is not right and the other wrong, they are simply different. You must account for the differences between your and your fiancé(e)'s patterns to communicate effectively.

   a. Place an X where you think you fall on the continuum and put an O where you think your fiancé(e) falls.

PATTERN OF EXPRESSION CONTINUUM
Fact-Oriented   **Feeling-Oriented**

1	2	3	4	5	6	7	8	9	10

Rational and logical   Emotional and random

1	2	3	4	5	6	7	8	9	10

Thinks "bottom-line"   Thinks "this is how I feel"

| 1 | 2 | 3 | 4 | 5 | 6 | 7 | 8 | 9 | 10 |

Difficulty expressing emotions   Passionate and expressive

b. Discuss your answer with your fiancé(e). Do you agree or disagree?

c. Describe a past discussion between you and your fiancé(e) in which your differences or similarities in pattern of expression were obvious.
Who said what?

_____

_____

_____

_____

How was it said?

_____

_____

_____

_____

What happened?

_____

_____

_____

_____

3. How was conflict resolved in your family as you grew up?

_____

_____

_____

_____

_____

4. Which of the four conflict resolution styles do you adopt in most conflicts?

    ❑ Fight to win   ❑ Yield
    ❑ Withdraw   ❑ Lovingly resolve

5. Which of the four styles does your *fiancé(e)* usually adopt in conflicts?

    ❑ Fight to win   ❑ Yield
    ❑ Withdraw   ❑ Lovingly resolve

6. Have you seen unresolved conflict damage your relationship? How?

    _____

    _____

    _____

    _____

7. Do you feel you have trouble admitting fault? Does your fiancé(e)?

    _____

    _____

    _____

    _____

8. Do you have trouble expressing forgiveness? Does your fiancé(e)?

    _____

    _____

9. Communication Exercise: Share Your Life Map
    Take turns explaining your Life Maps from the Personal History Worksheet.

    Keep in mind the principles you've already learned about authentic communication as you review your fiancé(e)'s Life

Map. Remember, don't just hear the words, but discern tone of voice and nonverbal clues. Make sure you use clarifying and summary questions when appropriate. Finally, be sure your focus as a listener is on the right things.

Here are a few questions to ask about the major milestones your fiancé(e) describes in the Life Map:

- How did that make you feel then?
- How does that make you feel now?
- What do you think God wants you to do with that?
- How do you think that event shaped your view of yourself—physically, intellectually, socially and/or spiritually?
- Do you think you are still carrying emotions from that event today?
- In what ways did these things shape your dreams and desires?
- In what ways did these things shape your fears and anxieties?
- What have you learned from these experiences?
- In what ways are you who you are today because of these events?
- How do you see your relationship fitting into the ebb and flow of your Life Map?

get to the heart of your marriage—prayer

No doubt, by this point you are well aware of the spiritual nature of marriage. In this area of communication, it should come as no surprise that your communication with God will have a direct influence on your communication with your fiancé(e).

In this time of prayer, practice your listening skills by praying back to God what you hear Him saying in His Word to you.

1. As you kneel together, read the following verses silently to yourself:

How blessed is the man who does not walk in the counsel of the wicked, nor stand in the path of sinners, nor sit in the seat of scoffers!

But his delight is in the law of the LORD, and in His law he meditates day and night.

And he will be like a tree firmly planted by streams of water, which yields its fruit in its season, and its leaf does not wither; and in whatever he does, he prospers (Psalm 1:1-3).

2. After a few moments of silently reading and thinking about the verse, one of you should read the verse aloud.

3. Now say a prayer to God that reflects back to Him what was expressed in this psalm.

Example:
Dear God,

You say in Psalm 1 that a blessed person is someone who is serious about knowing and obeying Your Word. I want to be a person like that. Rather than listening to what others say, help me to listen to what You say. In Christ's name, amen.

get deeper

Here are two special optional assignments for those who want to go deeper:

1. Read pages 201-209 in *Staying Close* by Dennis Rainey.

2. Complete the Couple's Interview Project (at the end of this session).

questions for those who were previously married

1. In what ways do you think poor communication contributed to the failure of your first marriage? Bottom line, what mistakes did *you* make in the area of communication? (Look back at the principles learned in this session.)

    _____

    _____

    _____

    _____

    _____

    _____

2. List some reasons why you believe you will not make the same communication mistakes in this marriage.

    _____

    _____

    _____

    _____

    _____

3. What specific changes do you think you need to make in your communication style as you consider remarriage?

    _____

    _____

    _____

    _____

    _____

What skills do you need to develop and practice? Review the principles learned in this session.

_____

_____

_____

_____

_____

_____

BONUS

Couple's Interview Project

Hearing from others who have gone before you is one of the most rewarding and beneficial things you can do for your engagement and your marriage. This project will help you do just that. You are going to discover what seeds you need to be planting now to have a colorful, fragrant and vibrant marriage 5, 10, 20 years down the road.

INSTRUCTIONS

1. Complete this interview with your mentor couple or another married couple (married at least five years) that you both respect and admire.

2. Ask this couple if they would spend some time with you to complete an interview that is part of your premarital counseling. Explain that the interview consists of seven questions about marriage and family life. The questions are simple and straightforward so they won't need any preparation time.

3. Conduct the interview over dinner, dessert or coffee. You may want to take turns asking the questions. If you have other questions you'd like to ask them, be sure to ask their permission.

4. Remember to employ the communication skills you have just learned.

    ♥ Ask clarifying and summary questions.
    ♥ Listen for the total message (words, tone, nonverbal clues).

5. Take notes. The insights you gain in this time will be invaluable. We guarantee it!

Looking Back

1. Describe how you met and got engaged.
   What was life like for you?

   _____

   _____

   _____

   _____

   What attracted you to each other?

   _____

   _____

   _____

   _____

   How did you propose?

   _____

   _____

   _____

   _____

   What were some of the emotions you felt at various points
   in the process?

   _____

   _____

   _____

   _____

2. What are some of the fondest memories you have of your first
   years of marriage? Why?

   _____

   _____

   _____

   _____

3. What were the greatest areas of conflict or tension in your first
    few years of marriage? How did you handle them?

    _____

    _____

    _____

    _____

4. How has your relationship with God affected your communica-
    tion with one another?

    _____

    _____

    _____

    _____

5. What is the most important lesson you've learned about com-
    munication since your marriage?

    _____

    _____

    _____

    _____

Looking at the Present

1. What have you learned about your spouse that has been *most
    helpful* to you as you seek to understand and love each other?

    _____

    _____

    _____

    _____

2. What are the greatest areas of conflict in your marriage today?

    _____

    _____

    _____

    _____

What spiritual principles have been most helpful to you in solving these tensions?

_____

_____

_____

_____

3. How do you manage schedules, work demands and outside activities while maintaining family and your time together as a priority?

_____

_____

_____

_____

4. What are some practical ways you have found to keep your relationship with God a priority in your marriage and family?

_____

_____

_____

_____

Looking Ahead

What advice would you give us today that you think will make the greatest difference in our marriage 20 years from now?

_____

_____

_____

_____

"For two people in a marriage to live together day after day is unquestionably the one miracle the Vatican has overlooked."

—BILL COSBY

Session Four

RoLes aND ResPonsIbILITIes:
movInG Beyond CuLturaL Stereotypes

true NortH

THE BIBLE SETS FORTH SPECIFIC
AND DISTINCT ROLES FOR A
HUSBAND AND WIFE THAT MUST
BE ACCURATELY UNDERSTOOD
AND PRACTICALLY FULFILLED.

You're driving down a street and from behind you comes the driving, thudding sound of music. A teenage driver has decided to give everyone within 500 yards the pleasure of listening to his music. You wonder how this kid could drive, or even think, with his music turned up so loud.

Discussing roles in marriage is like that. If you try to calmly explain a workable model of the roles to someone, the noise of our culture may easily drown you out. Many people don't even like the word "roles"—to them it's the *R* word never to be spoken in enlightened circles. They prefer to view the ideal marriage as a 50/50 relationship.

The irony is that every marriage settles into some type of social and organizational arrangement with both husband and wife playing specific roles to uphold it. The bottomline is *there are no roleless marriages*. But because the noise of our culture is so loud and confusing on this issue, few people know what those roles should be or how they should work. In the midst of this confusion, God has clearly spoken through His Word about how a marriage is to work.

As you complete this session, you will be given the opportunity to intentionally and biblically think about and plan your God-given roles as a husband or wife. In doing so, you'll begin to see the benefits of building your marriage on God's unchanging design.

 # ǥet the picture

1. In the past, what were the traditional roles for a husband and wife, as many people understood them?

   _____

   _____

   _____

   _____

2. Now think for a moment about how the media, especially television and films, generally portray husbands and wives.

a. Which of the following characters best describe, in your view, how *wives* are portrayed today? Think of an example, if possible. (Feel free to check more than one character.)

❑ The Heroine   ❑ The Martyr
❑ The Victim   ❑ The Extra
❑ The Villain   ❑ The Leader
❑ The Brain   ❑ The Tyrant
❑ Other_____

Example:

b. Which of the following characters best describe, in your view, how *husbands* are portrayed today? Think of an example, if possible. (Feel free to check more than one character.)

❑ The Hero   ❑ The Martyr
❑ The Incompetent Idiot   ❑ The Extra
❑ The Villain   ❑ The Pioneering Explorer
❑ The Brawn (no brain)   ❑ The Leader
❑ The Tyrant
❑ Other _____

Example:

3. Rank how each of the following influenced your understanding of roles in marriage. Use number 1 to represent the *most* influential voice. Use number 6 to represent the *least* influential voice.

_____ How I saw my parents live out their marriage
_____ What I have observed from today's culture
_____ How my peers have chosen to live out their marriages
_____ What I've learned from the Bible and church
_____ Things I have read, studied, seen, etc.
_____ Other_____

4.   What effect has confusion about roles had on marriages today?

_____

_____

_____

_____

In the past our culture has viewed the man's role as the "head of the household." He was seen as the leader, authority figure, decision-maker, wage-earner, indoor-outdoor maintenance man and chief disciplinarian. His word was law.

The woman's traditional role was to "submit" to her husband. She served her husband by keeping the household orderly and clean. She cooked and she cared for the children. She acquiesced to his will and did not question his decisions.

In our culture today, however, we see a backlash against these traditional roles. The idea that the man should be the leader in a marriage is seen as unjust, confining, cruel and antiquated. And the feminist movement has succeeded in convincing new generations of women to seek fulfillment in their careers. The woman who stays at home with her children is portrayed as unintelligent, boring and wasting her time doing housework.

As women become more assertive, many men become increasingly passive in their homes. At the same time, our society grows more sexually ambiguous. Boys and girls grow up with little concept of what it means to be a man or woman.

The tragedy is that when people today rebel against roles, they are actually arguing against the traditional stereotype. Even the *traditional* roles as practiced in our society were quite different from true *biblical* roles.

It's time to learn what the Bible really says.

get the truth

Let's do a quick review.

As we consider what the Bible has to say about role responsibilities in marriage, it is important to remember that these roles are not arbitrary or cultural. These are not positions that denote privilege or rank, but rather *functions* in the context of teamwork—functions that are inseparably tied to God's purposes for marriage. Roles are part of God's perfect design.

In marriage, both husband and wife have distinct "core roles" and "core responses." We will examine each separately. In preparation, we need to define these terms.

Key Terms Defined

A **Core Role** is an *essential function* that God has given husbands or wives to fulfill in a marriage relationship.

A **Core Response** is the *primary response* that God requires from men or women in order to enable and encourage their spouses to fulfill their core roles.

A Very Important Announcement

There is great misunderstanding about the roles of men and women today. Therefore, when we discuss core roles for men and women in marriage, it's important that you not jump to conclusions about what this session will teach. When you finish working through the material, you may find you have a different perspective on what the Bible says about this subject.

In *Building Teamwork in Your Marriage*, part of the HomeBuilders Couples Series® Bible Study Electives, Robert Lewis writes:

> The titles selected for a husband's role and a wife's role...should be considered as core roles and not comprehensive lifestyles. In other words, these roles for husbands and wives, though essential to a marriage, are not all one does in the marriage....There is great latitude, creativity, and flexibility around one's core role. There is also great danger in ignoring these core roles, altering them or violating them.[1]

God's Core Role for a Husband: Servant-Leader

1. Read the following verses and underline the word "head" each time it is used.

    "For the husband is the head of the wife, as Christ also is the head of the church, He Himself being the Savior of the body" (Ephesians 5:23).

    "Now I praise you because you remember me in everything, and hold firmly to the traditions, just as I delivered them to you. But I want you to understand that Christ is the head of every man, and the man is the head of a woman, and God is the head of Christ" (1 Corinthians 11:2,3).

    a. According to the Ephesians passage quoted above, who should be the model for a husband's servant-leadership?

        _____

        _____

        _____

    b. Why do you think it is important that a man understand that his "headship" (leadership) is to be like that of Christ?

        _____

        _____

        _____

2. What key words or phrases describe the two types of leaders in the following passage?

    "And calling them to Himself, Jesus said to them, 'You know that those who are recognized as rulers of the Gentiles lord it over them; and their great men exercise authority over them. But it is not so among you, but whoever wishes to become great among you shall be your servant; and whoever wishes to be first among you shall be slave of all. For even the Son of Man did not come to be served, but to serve, and to give His life a ransom for many'" (Mark 10:42-45).

Jesus' Leadership	Gentile Leadership

3. What additional insight can you gain from the following passage about what it means for a man to lead his wife?

    "Husbands, love your wives, just as Christ also loved the church and gave Himself up for her" (Ephesians 5:25).

    _____

    _____

    _____

    _____

In the marriage relationship, God calls the husband to be a servant-leader. This is his core role. His leadership should model that of Jesus. A servant-leader serves like Christ and loves like Christ! He is a mix of both servant and leader.

Being a servant-leader does _not_ mean...

♥   Becoming a lording leader, making all the decisions himself or selfishly seeking to control others so he can meet his own needs.

♥   A man must be outgoing and have a "rally-the-troops" personality.

♥   He becomes a passive non-leader, disengaged relationally, giving little or no direction to his wife and family.

♥   A man cannot delegate or a wife cannot initiate.

Being a servant-leader _does_ mean...

♥   The husband assumes overall responsibility for the direction of his family, and takes the intitiative to serve the needs of his wife and family.

♥   He assumes responsibility to maximize his wife's gifts and abilities.

- He pours out his life on his wife's behalf so she can become all that God intended.
- He denies himself and gives of his life on behalf of his wife and family.

Here is a key phrase, that if embraced and practiced, will enable you to provide servant-leadership in your marriage and family:

TAKE THE INITIATIVE!

- *Take the initiative* to be the spiritual leader in the home— to pray, to worship at church, and to study God's Word.
- *Take the initiative* to see that finances are in order, needs are met and your wife feels financially secure.
- *Take the initiative* to ask forgiveness, resolve conflict and ensure your home is a place of encouragement and safety.

4. Complete the chart on the following page that contrasts the way a servant-leader, a lording-leader and a passive non-leader would handle everyday situations at home.

SITUATION	LORDING LEADER	PASSIVE NON-LEADER	SERVANT-LEADER
The couple needs to purchase a new automobile.	*He buys what he wants without considering what his wife and family need.*	*He puts off the discussion and the decision. He leaves all the shopping and research up to his wife, then becomes non-communicative or angry when he doesn't like the choice.*	*He deliberates with his wife, making a joint decision based on both of their input and desires. He puts the needs of the family before his own personal preference.*
The husband arrives home and the house is messy and dinner is not prepared.			
Facing a huge bill for car repairs, the couple grows discouraged about whether God will provide for their needs.			
The husband wants to go camping in the mountains for vacation, but the wife prefers going to a beach resort.			

A word to the men: Assuming the role of servant-leader is a weighty responsibility that will challenge you to become all God intended. Your faithful commitment to love your wife and family through servant-leadership will prove to be one of the greatest privileges of your life.

Core Response of the Wife to the Husband's Role: Submission

Read the following passage:

> Wives, be subject to your own husbands, as to the Lord. For the husband is the head of the wife, as Christ also is the head of the church, He Himself being the Savior of the body. But as the church is subject to Christ, so also the wives ought to be to their husbands in everything (Ephesians 5:22-24).

Note that this passage does not call on wives to *obey* their husbands, but to *be subject*. Submission means empowering the husband to be the leader; it is a wife's core response to her husband's servant-leadership.

The appeal in verse 22 is ultimately an issue between a woman and her Lord. Husbands are never told to order their wives to submit, but to love and lead them in such a way that makes it easy for them to do so voluntarily.

5.   Can you think of some reasons that all of us find it difficult to submit to other people in various situations of life?

_____

_____

_____

_____

6.   **For women only**: Does an accurate definition of the man's core role as servant-leader make the thought of submission easier and more reasonable? Why or why not?

_____

_____

_____

Remember, submission is a woman's response to her husband, *not* her core role. It is the response that encourages a husband to fulfill his core role as a servant-leader.

A Word of Caution

The principle of submission never includes being asked to disobey other scriptural principles. A man's leadership over his wife is meant to fulfill the Scripture in their marriage, not to violate it.

God's Core Role for a Wife: Helper-Homemaker

Read the following verses:

> Then the LORD God said, "It is not good for the man to be alone; I will make him a helper suitable for him" (Genesis 2:18).

> Older women likewise are to be reverent in their behavior, not malicious gossips, nor enslaved to much wine, teaching what is good, that they may encourage the young women to love their husbands, to love their children, to be sensible, pure, workers at home, kind, being subject to their own husbands, that the word of God may not be dishonored (Titus 2:3-5).

7. In Hebrews 13:6, we are told, "The LORD is my helper, I will not be afraid." How does knowing that God describes Himself as our helper change the way a wife could feel about being called "a helper"?

_____

_____

_____

_____

An accurate understanding of the role of a wife as helper shows how vital the role is in providing what the husband needs to complete himself. Husbands have gaps in their lives that their wives are uniquely qualified to fill.

8. **For men:** What are some ways you need your fiancée's help?

    _____

    _____

    _____

    _____

    For women: What are some ways your fiancé needs your help?

    _____

    _____

    _____

    _____

The opposite of being a helper is being a competitor. Competitors do the opposite of filling gaps and supporting weak areas. They exploit those weaknesses to gain the upperhand. A competitive wife stirs a man to aggression and retaliation or to withdrawal rather than caring, supporting and meeting the woman's need.

9. The word translated as "encourage" that Paul uses in Titus 2:4 literally means "train." So Paul is instructing older women to train young wives in domestic opportunities and responsibilities. What do you think it means to be a worker at home?

    _____

    _____

    _____

    _____

These words were just as radical in the first century as they are now. Historian Will Durant writes about biblical times:

> Emancipation [for women] was as complete then as now...Women worked in shops, or factories, especially in the textile trades; some became lawyers and doctors; some

became politically powerful; the decay of the ancient faith among the upper classes had washed away the supernatural supports of marriage, fidelity, and parentage; the passage from farm to city had made children less of an asset, more of a liability, and a toy; women wished to be sexually beautiful rather than maternally beautiful."[2]

Addressing this audience, Paul called women to make their homes the focus of their lives rather than their careers.

10. Why do you think so many women today believe that building a career is more fulfilling than being a homemaker and raising children?

_____

_____

_____

_____

11. Our culture often labels homemakers as weak, unfulfilled women who have no joy or purpose in life. But in light of what you've learned about God's purposes and plans for marriage, why do you think He desires for a wife and mother to be focused on being a worker at home?

_____

_____

_____

_____

Notice how Paul concludes the passage in Titus with the warning: "that the word of God may not be dishonored" (Titus 2:5).

Paul's conclusion teaches us that his instructions in this area are not just for the women of the first century. Because God's Word does not pass out of fashion, an issue as central as bringing honor or dishonor to His Word is an issue that transcends cultural fads and trends.

At stake here is an organizational structure that God created to make a marriage work. God designed a woman as a completer for her husband. Man is to be a self-denying servant-leader of his wife and family. When a husband and wife are fulfilling these roles in marriage, they honor and glorify God.

The Core Response of the Husband to the Wife's Core Role: Praise and Honor

12. In the following verses, circle the words that describe the kind of *core* response a wife needs from her husband.

     "Her husband...praises her, saying: 'Many daughters have done nobly, but you excel them all'" (Proverbs 31:28,29).

     "Grant her honor as a fellow heir of the grace of life" (1 Peter 3:7).

13. **For men only**: Why is your core response of praise and honor so crucial to the success of your fiancée pursuing her biblical role?

     _____

     _____

     _____

     _____

     What will happen if she doesn't receive it from you?

     _____

     _____

     _____

     _____

Praise and honor are the masculine counterpart to submission. It is the core response of praise and honor that encourages and enables a wife to fulfill her calling as a helper-homemaker.

How a woman views her husband and her home is not only a statement of her values but also the source of her values. It is clear from Scripture that a wife plays a unique role in her husband's success as a man. He needs a helper and without his wife's special attention, he is prone to imbalance and blind spots. It is equally clear that God intended for the home and those within it to be a woman's core concern. Though a husband is called to provide for and manage a home, it is the wife's special calling to make it a home. These divine challenges are at the heart of her calling as a wife.

NaviGatinG by true North

TRUTHS TO CHART YOUR COURSE

- Every marriage settles into some type of social and organizational arrangement, with both husband and wife playing specific roles to uphold it. Bottom line: *there are no roleless marriages.*

- The Bible sets forth specific and distinct roles and responsibilities for a husband and wife in marriage.

- A core role is an essential function that God has given a man or woman to fulfill in a marriage relationship.

- A core response is the primary response God requires of a man or woman that enables and encourages his or her spouse to fulfill his or her core role.

- Roles address one's responsibility, not one's value. Both husband and wife are of equal value and worth before God and one another.

- The *core role* of a husband is to be a servant-leader, leading as Christ leads and loving as Christ loves. The wife's *core response* to this leadership is submission.

- The *core role* for a wife is to be a helper-homemaker, filling the gaps in her husband's life and prioritizing her life around home and family. The husband's *core response* to his wife is praise and honor.

1. Robert Lewis, *Building Teamwork in Your Marriage Bible Study Elective* (Ventura, Calif.: Gospel Light, 1995), p. 116.
2. Will Durant, *The Story of Civilization: Caesar and Christ, Vol. III* (New York: Simon & Schuster, 1944), p. 222, 370.

Couple's Project

get real

Interact as a couple around the following activities.

1. Spend a few minutes going through "Get the Picture" and "Get the Truth," sharing and discussing your answers to the different questions. Be sure to ask your fiancé(e) to explain the answers.

2. Based on what you've learned, write a definition for each of the following terms:
    Servant-leader

    Helper-homemaker

3. What roles did your parents assume in the home when you were growing up?

    a. Who was the leader in the marriage?

        _____

        _____

    b. Who was the leader as a parent?

        _____

        _____

    c. How did they make decisions?

        _____

        _____

4. At this time, how well do you believe you and your fiancé(e) are in agreement with God's design for a husband's and wife's distinct and specific roles?

    Not Aligned   Very Aligned
    1   2   3   4   5   6   7   8   9   10

Explain:

_____

_____

_____

5. Experiencing the *positive* power of core roles fulfilled:
    a. **Men:** Tell your fiancée about a time you realized she was a helper who filled gaps in your life. How did it make you feel?

    _____

    _____

    _____

    b. **Women:** Tell your fiancé about a time you realized he was a servant-leader who took the initiative for your good. How did it make you feel?

    _____

    _____

    _____

6. Experiencing the *negative* power of core roles unfulfilled:
    a. **Men:** Tell your fiancée about a time you felt she was more of a "competitor" than a helper. How did it make you feel?

    _____

    _____

    _____

b. **Women:** Tell your fiancé about a time you needed him to take the initiative but he did not. *Or* a time when you felt he was a lording leader or passive non-leader rather than a servant-leader. How did it make you feel?

_____

_____

_____

_____

7. Conflict over roles in marriage often centers on two areas: making important decisions and dividing household responsibilities. What insights have you gained in this session that could help you avoid conflict in these areas?

_____

_____

_____

_____

get to the Heart of your marriage—prayer

Only by the power of God will you be able to fulfill your core role and core response as either a servant-leader who praises his wife, or as a helper-homemaker who submits to her husband.

1. Take a few moments and using the sample prayer as a springboard, pray together, expressing your desire to fulfill the unique role God has given each of you in marriage. Rather than praying for your fiancé(e) to fulfill his or her role, pray for yourself, that you would take responsibility in your role and your response.

2. Here is a sample of what the man might pray:

Dear God,
The high and privileged role You have called me to as a

servant-leader is something I want to strive for. There are many areas I need to develop in and many areas I need to take more responsibility for. Help me to love _____fiancé(e)'s name_____ as Christ loved the church and to serve her sacrificially. Bring to mind ways that I can praise and esteem her as my future helpmate. In Christ's name, Amen.

get Deeper

Here are two special optional assignments for those who want to go deeper:
1. Complete the Roles Position Statement (pages 183-185).
2. For a more in-depth look at roles, read *Rocking the Roles* by Robert Lewis and William Hendricks (NavPress, 1991). This resource is also available through FamilyLife at 1-800-FL-TODAY.

questions for those who were previously married

Answer the following questions individually then share your answers with your fiancé(e).
1. How were role responsibilities handled in your previous marriage?

_____

_____

_____

_____

2. Can you think of some ways that your view and practice of role responsibilities in your previous marriage are affecting your current relationship?

    _____

    _____

    _____

    _____

3. List at least three specific things you will do in this marriage to fulfill your biblical role responsibility that you may have failed to do in your previous marriage.

    _____

    _____

    _____

    _____

BONUS

ROLES POSITION Statement

The issue of roles in marriage is a volatile subject. Knowing *what* you believe about role responsibilities in marriage and *why* you believe it is one of the strongest statements you will make as a couple to the world around you.

This project will provide you the opportunity to formulate and formalize what you believe about this critical subject. Developing a clear, concise statement of belief will prove to be a refuge and an encouragement as you seek to build your marriage according to God's design.

Chances are this will not be the only time you will grapple with these issues. You may want to work through this project again after you are married and have some experience in working out your roles and responsibilities.

INSTRUCTIONS
1. Individually, prepare a Position Statement on two topics:

    ♥ What you believe about roles in marriage. Include biblical references that support *why* you believe as you do.
    ♥ How you will live those beliefs out in your marriage. Make this very practical.

2. Refer back to your notes in this session to formulate your position.
3. Try to make each section a short and concise paragraph. Both statements, written out, should not exceed a half sheet of paper.
4. After you have completed your own personal statement, meet

with your fiancé(e) to compare your positions. Together, hammer out a statement that the two of you can agree represents what you, together, believe about roles in marriage. This position statement will begin "We believe..."

ROLES IN MARRIAGE

What We Believe

How Our Beliefs Will Be Lived Out in Our Marriage

_____   _____
                signature   date

_____   _____
                signature   date

_____   _____
            witness signature   date

"There are three conversions: the conversion of the
heart, the mind and the purse."

— MARTIN LUTHER

money, money, money

true north

GOD OWNS IT ALL, AND WE ARE
STEWARDS OF HIS RESOURCES.

Finances can be to marriage what a match is to gasoline—explosive!
Generally, it is a disagreement about how money should or shouldn't
be spent that creates the spark that starts the fire that grows in inten-
sity until the marriage is engulfed in a seemingly irreversible firestorm.

From God's perspective, however, money should create a spark
of a different sort. This spark of understanding, when fanned by
the commitment to do God's will together, can blaze into the real-
ization that you have the incredible privilege and responsibility of
managing His money for His eternal purposes. And that blaze can

develop into a holy fire that is committed to God's purposes, having a positive effect on every area of your marriage.

Christian couples work most of their lives at communicating with one another about what it means to be stewards of what God has given them. Decisions on spending, saving, giving, investing, hobbies, allowances and many other related issues are all hammered out over the years together.

We don't want to spoil all the fun before your marriage (you need a few surprises to work out together!), but many of you probably find managing your finances a challenge even as a single person. You can save yourselves a great deal of conflict after the wedding day if you discuss a few key issues now.

In this session you will uncover the secrets of true contentment when it comes to money and material possessions. You will have the opportunity as a couple to think through your attitudes, hopes and plans in this critical area of finances. This session won't solve the future challenges you'll face around money, but it will give you some foundational truths and basic skills you need to apply to your lives.

get the picture

Read the following case study and respond to the questions that follow.

Case Study: Bob and Sherry's Financial Adventure

Bob and Sherry's financial challenges began as newyweds. Each day as they drove home from work to their small apartment, they passed a slick billboard. It pictured a beautiful home with the bold statement, "YOUR FAMILY DESERVES THE BEST."

With many of their friends buying homes in the new Mercer Lake development and with the housing market looking good, it seemed like a great time to buy a home. Their friends reinforced this idea with comments like, "Boy, it's great to be out of our old apartment!" and "How do you manage to live in such a cramped space?" Sherry kept telling Bob, "It sure would be nice to have a place of our own."

One day they heard that their wedding photos were ready. That night after work, Bob and Sherry eagerly rushed down to the studio to pick up the album. The pictures looked great and brought back many wonderful memories of their wedding day. However, the sting came when Bob looked at the photographer's bill. He began to feel the pressure of other bills that they were facing from their wedding and honeymoon in Cancun: hotels, airfare, restaurants, cruise line and gifts. But Bob didn't say anything about it to Sherry; he didn't want to spoil a great moment.

Sherry, meanwhile, was feeling a different pressure. Thanksgiving was coming, and her family would be joining them for the day. Since Sherry loved to entertain she wanted to make sure their house was in order. It really would be nice, she thought, if they could complete their set of china. "Bob, we could finish the set with just $300. In fact, that would allow us to entertain more often." Bob thought again of the other bills he hadn't mentioned to Sherry, but agreed to let her spend the money.

In the months ahead Bob started to feel their finances were getting away from them. Their credit cards bills were running up with furniture and clothing purchases.

"Sherry, we have got to try a budget!" Bob said. But after a couple of months, they gave up keeping track of their expenses, and they finally set the budget notebook aside. "It's too tedious," Bob moaned.

In late spring they received an offer of a $75 gift certificate to a department store, plus dinner for two at a nice restaurant. All they needed to do is to take a two-hour tour with a real-estate agent at the Mercer Lake development. They agreed to take the tour so they could receive the free gifts.

During the tour they were extremely impressed with the property. It looked like a wonderful place to have a home. The agent mentioned that homes were on sale at a "special low price" but only for that day. He also said they could even stretch out a down payment over 90 days at a low interest rate.

They talked for a few minutes and decided, "We'll get by somehow. Besides if we have to sell at a later date we will make a profit. We've got to take some risks to get ahead." They announced to the agent, "We'll take it."

"Great," he said. "You won't regret it."

In the next five months they began to quarrel more and more about money. Sherry believed Bob was spending too much money on frivolous purchases for himself. In anger he turned the finances over to Sherry, "If you are so smart, you take care of the bills!"

Then a golden opportunity came. Bob was offered a promotion at work. The salary was much higher, but it meant he would be away working longer hours.

The mortgage on the house was stretching them, but with both salaries they could make it and even eat out a couple of times each week. Then one day, Sherry asked Bob a question that would change their lives forever, "Bob, do you think we should paint the extra bedroom pink or blue?"

They celebrated the news of her pregnancy at their favorite restaurant and caught a late movie. On the drive home Bob pondered the thought of a little boy to play golf with someday. Sherry smiled to herself, imagining a little girl playing dolls and serving make-believe tea.

But in the quietness of the car and the cool evening breeze, a nagging question disturbing both of them: *How will we make it if Sherry has to stop working?*

1. How common do you think Bob and Sherry's scenario is for newly married couples?

   ❑ Uncommon, maybe true for one out of 10 couples;
   ❑ Common, true for probably half of the couples getting married today;
   ❑ Very common, most couples face a good bit of what Bob and Sherry experienced.

Why?

_____

_____

_____

_____

2. List some of the mistakes you think Bob and Sherry made along the way.

_____

_____

_____

_____

3. Make your own list of the financial mistakes you think you could most likely make in your first years of marriage. These can be attitudes, actions or beliefs.
   My Top Five Concerns:

   a. _____

   b. _____

   c. _____

   d. _____

   e. _____

The mistakes Bob and Sherry made were all too common for married couples. Many people become adults with little training in how to handle money. They don't know how to set priorities, they are influenced by the culture and their peers, and they lack the basic discipline they need to set and keep a budget. Most importantly, they lack God's perspective on finances.

get the truth

When discussing finances, there are two foundational questions you must answer to gain a biblical perspective on money. Without them, you are left to the winds of culture, the Madison Avenue ads and the impulsive and unpredictable passions of your heart to guide you.

Who Does this Money Belong to Anyway?

1. Read the following passages and circle the phrases indicating who owns our money:

   "The earth is the LORD's and all it contains, the world, and those who dwell in it" (Psalm 24:1).

   " 'Thine, O LORD, is the greatness and the power and the glory and the victory and the majesty, indeed everything that is in the heavens, and the earth; Thine is the dominion, O LORD, and Thou dost exalt Thyself as head over all. Both riches and honor come from Thee...For all things come from Thee, and from Thy hand we have given Thee. O LORD our God, all this abundance that we have provided to build Thee a house for Thy holy name, it is from Thy hand, and all is Thine' " (1 Chronicles 29:11,12,14,16).

2. How should the truth that *God owns everything* affect the way you view material possessions and financial resources? Give a specific example of how you should apply this in your marriage.

   _____

   _____

   _____

   _____

3.   Critique the following statement:

"I'll give God 10 percent of my income and spend the other 90 percent as I please."

_____

_____

_____

_____

It is natural and human to feel that what we earn is ours, and we don't need to answer to anyone else. But the Scriptures we've studied make it clear that the first foundational truth we must embrace is that God owns it all.

If God Is the Owner, What Does that Make Me?

4.   What does the following passage say about our responsibility for the resources God has given us?

"'He who is faithful in a very little thing is faithful also in much; and he who is unrighteous in a very little thing is unrighteous also in much. If therefore you have not been faithful in the use of unrighteous mammon, who will entrust the true riches to you? And if you have not been faithful in the use of that which is another's, who will give you that which is your own? No servant can serve two masters; for either he will hate the one, and love the other, or else he will hold to one, and despise the other. You cannot serve God and mammon'" (Luke 16:10-13).

_____

_____

_____

5. The second foundational truth regarding finances flows from the first. If God owns it all, then we are not owners—*we are stewards of His resources*. What are the marks of a steward according to the same passage?

    _____

    _____

    _____

    _____

6. A steward is a person who manages another's property, finances or other affairs, one who acts as a supervisor or administrator of finances or property for another.

    Based on this definition, fill in the corresponding trait of a *steward* as contrasted with an *owner*:

Owner	Steward
Answers to himself	Answers to the owner
Can do as he pleases	
Amount of possessions is what brings value and esteem	
He gets more by purchasing more	

7. Look again at the end of the Luke passage quoted in question 4. Why do you believe it is impossible for a person to serve both God and money?

    _____

    _____

    _____

    _____

8. Give an example of someone you've seen try to serve both God and money and what ultimately happened to that person.

_____

_____

_____

_____

9. If God owns it all and you are to be stewards of the resources He entrusts to you, which do you think best represents the perspective you should take towards your finances?

❑ The more money we make the better off we will be.

❑ It doesn't really matter how we manage our money—gee, it's not even ours.

❑ Since we don't have much, God can't expect much from us in this area.

❑ Our attitudes and actions regarding money have serious spiritual consequences.

❑ Some day when we have some money, we'll make sure we honor God with it.

Why?

_____

_____

_____

_____

Getting Practical

Because you are stewards of the resources God has entrusted to you, every financial decision you make is actually a spiritual decision. For many, that's a revolutionary concept. How you manage your finances is a pretty good barometer for the condition of your spiritual life.

10. Based on what you've learned in this session, how do you think you might apply those principles to each of the following areas?

a. Forming, maintaining and living within a budget

_____

_____

_____

_____

b. Cost of the wedding and honeymoon

_____

_____

_____

_____

c. Type of lifestyle you will lead as a couple after marriage

_____

_____

_____

_____

d. Giving to God's work

_____

_____

_____

_____

e. Debt

_____

_____

_____

_____

The fact is that knowing God's perspective on finances should influence every area of your money management. You will realize, for example, that you have a responsibility to live within the means God has given you. You will look closely at your attitudes about material possessions and be more strict about your purchases. And you will free up more resources to go toward making God's work possible.

11. Rate yourself and your fiancé(e) on the following two statements:
    a. My present attitude and practice reflect the biblical truths that God owns it all and I am a steward of the resources He entrusts to me.

Poorly reflect   Strongly reflect
1   2   3   4   5   6   7   8   9   10

Why?

_____

_____

_____

    b. My fiancé(e)'s attitude and practice reflect the biblical truths that God owns it all and he or she is a steward of the resources God has entrusted to him or her.

Poorly reflect   Strongly reflect
1   2   3   4   5   6   7   8   9   10

Why?

_____

_____

_____

In the context of these truths—that God owns it all and we are stewards of His resources—you will hammer out money issues over a lifetime. While developing a biblical view of finances together as a team, you will experience one of the great privileges and joys of marriage.

navigating by true north

TRUTHS TO CHART YOUR COURSE

- God owns it all and we are stewards of His resources.
- There is no such thing as an independent financial decision. Each decision you make will influence every future financial decision.
- Money is not an end in itself. It is a tool to be used to accomplish God's plans and purposes.
- Our attitude about money will drive our actions regarding money.
- The root issue in finances is never the amount of money; it is the attitude we have towards money.

Couple's Project

get real

1. Spend a few minutes sharing and discussing your answers to the questions in "Get the Picture" and "Get the Truth." Be sure to ask your fiancé(e) to explain his or her answers.

2. In the chart that follows, make checkmarks beside the statements that best describe you and your fiancé(e). Then share your answers and discuss potential areas of conflict.

You		Your Fiancé(e)
	I'll buy it when I need it.	
	Buy it now while it's on sale and save.	
	K-Mart, blue light specials, generic is the way to go!	
	Malls, specialty boutiques—I only go for name brands.	
	Gas is gas; who cares where you buy it?	
	Gas is three cents cheaper down the street.	
	I'm within $50 of reconciling the checkbook this month—awesome!!	
	I'm not spending anything else until I discover that nickel discrepancy between my checkbook and the bank statement.	
	We shouldn't go to the movies tonight because we've spent our entertainment money for the month.	
	I'm a little over in this area of the budget, so I'm borrowing from next month.	

Most couples find that they differ significantly in a number of these areas. You have learned throughout this workbook that your differences are not a negative; in fact recall from Session One that your differences are what bond you together.

Your aim should not be to change your fiancé(e) so he or she approaches financial issues just like you. The aim is for both of you to work from the same financial understanding: God owns it all and we are stewards of His resources.

3. Write a brief statement about the most important insights you have gained about the biblical principles of money from this session.

    _____

    _____

    _____

    _____

4. Individually, make a list of seven material possessions that you value highly. Be specific (e.g., my stereo system, my savings, my car, my grandmother's china etc.). Then share your lists with each other.

    _____

    _____

    _____

    _____

 # get to the Heart of your marriage —prayer

1. Make a list of your current financial concerns, then lift each of these concerns up to God in prayer.

2. One way to acknowledge that indeed "God owns it all" is to express that fact in prayer. Take a moment right now and make a statement to God that you understand that these possessions

are in fact His possessions. Your prayer might sound something like this:

Lord, I want You to know that I believe You own everything, and that includes everything on my list. Because it is all Yours, I want to thank You for entrusting these things to me.

Each of you can join the other as you express this prayer to God.

get Deeper

1. Work through the Bonus Project on setting a budget (pp. 213-218). This project should only be done if you are engaged and within four months of your wedding date. Beginning to intermingle your finances prior to this is premature and could be unhealthy.

2. For more help on organizing your finances, we suggest reading *Money Before Marriage* by Larry Burkett with Michael E. Taylor, Moody Press, 1991.

questions for those who were previously married

Answer these questions individually and then share your answers with your fiancé(e).

1. What lessons did you learn about financial issues in your first marriage that will be helpful as you prepare to marry again?

   _____

   _____

   _____

   _____

2. In what ways will continuing financial obligations related to your first marriage affect your new marriage, and how will you handle these?

   _____

   _____

   _____

   _____

3. If you receive any type of financial support from a previous spouse, how will that income be handled in your new marriage?

   _____

   _____

   _____

   _____

4. Can you think of any material possessions from your previous marriage that might trouble your fiancé(e) that you need to discuss (home, pictures, sentimental objects etc.)?

   _____

   _____

   _____

   _____

BONUS

Setting a Budget

As you approach your wedding date, begin to set up a budget that will allow you to control your finances from the very beginning of your marriage. As you fill in the blanks, here are some key questions to ask yourself:

- Are you saving enough for long-term needs?
- Can you stay out of debt with this budget?
- What do you have to sacrifice in order to stick with this budget?
- If the wife becomes pregnant, could you live on the income of the husband?

Household Budget

Date	Monthly Income $		
Budget Category	**Monthly**	**Other than monthly**	**Total**
Housing			
Mortgage/rent			
Insurance			
Property taxes			
Electricity			
Gas			
Water			
Sanitation			
Cleaning			
Telephone			
Repairs/maintenance			
Supplies			
Other			
Total			

Budget Category	Monthly	Other than monthly	Total
Food			
Clothing			
Transportation			
Insurance			
Gas and oil			
Maintenance/repairs			
Parking			
Other			
Total			

Budget Category	Monthly	Other than monthly	Total
Entertainment/Recreation			
Eating out			
Movies, concerts, etc.			
Baby-sitters			
Magazines/newspapers			
Vacations			
Clubs/activities			
Other			
Total			

Budget Category	Monthly	Other than monthly	Total
Medical Expenses			
Doctor			
Dentist			
Insurance			
Medication			
Other			
Total			

Budget Category	Monthly	Other than monthly	Total
Other Insurance			
Life			
Disability			
Other			
Total			

Budget Category	Monthly	Other than monthly	Total
Children			
Tuition			
School lunches			
Allowances			
Lessons/activities			
Other			
Total			

Budget Category	Monthly	Other than monthly	Total
Gifts			
Christmas			
Birthdays			
Anniversaries			
Other			
Total			

Budget Category	Monthly	Other than monthly	Total
Miscellaneous			
Toiletries			
Husband misc.			
Wife misc.			
Cleaning, laundry			
Animal care			
Hair care			
Other			
Total			
Total Living Expenses			

"Contrary to [what some believe], sex is not a sin.
Contrary to Hugh Hefner, it's not salvation either.
Like nitroglycerin, it can be used either to
blow up bridges or to heal hearts."

— FREDRICK BUECHNER

"We feasted on love; every mode of it, solemn and
merry, romantic and realistic, sometimes as dramatic
as a thunderstorm, sometimes comfortable and unemphatic as putting on your soft slippers. She was my
pupil and my teacher, my subject and my sovereign,
my trusty comrade, friend, shipmate, fellow-soldier.
My mistress, but at the same time all that
any man friend has ever been to me."

— C.S. LEWIS

Intimacy: Sexual Communication in Marriage

true North
SEX IS GOD'S IDEA

Where would you expect to find the following article titles: "How to Maintain an Erotic Marriage"; "Five Sex Secrets Women Wish Husbands Knew"; "Sexual Limits—What Other Women Will (And Won't) Do in Bed"? In the Adults Only section of the newsstand? Try *Readers Digest* or *Redbook*!

Turn on the television and it's difficult to find the product in many commercials. Are they selling sex or cereal? Intimacy or instant coffee? Is this an advertisement for a Caribbean cruise or a steamy novel? It's hard to tell with copylines like, "There is no law that says you can't make love at four in the afternoon on a Tuesday."

Sex has become a cultural obsession, but the picture of sex that our culture paints is a cheap counterfeit and a perversion of God's original design. Like a surgeon's knife that has been designed for good, but can be used for harm if put in the wrong hands, sex has been twisted and torn from its original purposes with devastating consequences.

In this session, you will catch a glimpse of the incredible power and privilege that God has given us in sexual intimacy. You'll uncover some possible misconceptions and replace them with God's perspective from the Scriptures. You will have the opportunity to talk about some of your fears and expectations. And you will gain an appreciation for your unique God-given design as a man or a woman and how your differences in this area will continue to strengthen your marriage bond.

Important Instructions

If possible, this session should be completed in the presence of a mentor, pastor or counselor. Also, before proceeding, take a few minutes to read the special section at the end of this session beginning on page 226: "The Past: How Much Do I Share?" It will give you some guidelines on the appropriate level of disclosure regarding your past sexual experience. Don't proceed without reading it for your and your fiancé(e)'s sake.

get the picture

1. What percentage of your sex education was received at each of the following "institutions"? (Your total should equal 100 percent.)

_____% Peer School: My friends talked about what we thought, knew or had heard.

_____% Home School: My parents explained to me what sex is.

_____% Private School: I read things on my own or asked certain people (not my parents).

_____% Christian School: Church, Sunday School or youth group.

_____% School of Hard Knocks: I learned by experience.

_____% School of the Silver Screen: I learned from movies, videos or television.

_____% School of _____

100% Total

2. What are some of the *helpful* things that you learned in these schools?

_____

_____

_____

_____

3. What are some of the *harmful* things that you learned in these schools?

_____

_____

_____

_____

4. In our culture today, why do you think it is so important to learn what the Bible says about the sexual relationship?

_____

_____

_____

_____

The unfortunate fact is that most of us have received a poor sex education. Our knowledge, our viewpoints and our experiences are twisted by our culture; we learn about sex from man's perspective. In order to build a good sexual relationship when you are married, you need to learn what the Creator had in mind.

get the truth

Once again, let's return to Genesis for some clues about God's view of sex:

> "For this cause a man shall leave his father and his mother, and shall cleave to his wife; and they shall become one flesh" (Genesis 2:24).

The first perspective to notice here is that God created sex. This sounds like a simple statement, yet it is profound.

1. Give some reasons why viewing sex as part of God's original design for marriage is so important.

    _____

    _____

    _____

    _____

Now let's look at the term "one flesh." You will recall from Session Two that this phrase is the origin of the word "oneness." Becoming one flesh involves deep relational intimacy of which sexual intercourse is an integral part.

Review what Dr. Louis Evans, Jr. wrote about the term, "one flesh":

> The one flesh in marriage is not just a physical phenomenon, but a uniting of the totality of two personalities. In marriage, we are one flesh spiritually by vow, economically by sharing, logistically by adjusting time and agreeing on the disbursement of all life's resources, experientially by trudging through the dark valleys and standing victoriously on the peaks of success, and sexually by the bonding of our bodies.[1]

2. How does this perspective contrast with that of our culture today?

_____

_____

_____

_____

Sex is not just a physical act. God created it as a *process* of intimate communication with the act of physical intercourse becoming a significant part. It is a powerful, emotional bonding experience designed to strengthen marriage much as metal rods reinforce concrete.

Premarital sex is so common in our culture today that some people are considered old-fashioned, if not prudish, for maintaining their purity until marriage. But God has our best in mind when He commanded us to not engage in fornication. He wants us to experience the absolute best, rather than a poor counterfeit.

The Right Purposes

For each of the following verses, state in your own words the purpose you see that God has for sex in marriage.

PURPOSE NUMBER ONE

"And God blessed [Adam and Eve]; and God said to them, 'Be fruitful and multiply, and fill the earth' " (Genesis 1:28).

"Behold, children are a gift of the LORD; the fruit of the womb is a reward. Like arrows in the hand of a warrior, so are the children of one's youth. How blessed is the man whose quiver is full of them" (Psalm 127:3-5).

3.   According to these verses, one purpose God has for sex is...

_____

_____

_____

_____

PURPOSE NUMBER TWO

"Let your fountain be blessed, and rejoice in the wife of your youth. As a loving hind and a graceful doe, let her breasts satisfy you at all times; be exhilarated always with her love" (Proverbs 5:18,19).

4.   According to these verses, a second purpose God has for sex is...

_____

_____

_____

_____

PURPOSE NUMBER THREE

"But because of immoralities, let each man have his own wife, and let each woman have her own husband. Let the husband fulfill his duty to his wife, and likewise also the wife to her husband. The wife does not have authority over her own body, but the husband does; and likewise also the husband does not have authority over his own body, but the wife does. Stop depriving one another, except by agreement for a time that you may devote yourselves to prayer, and come together again lest Satan tempt you because of your lack of self-control" (1 Corinthians 7:2-5).

5.   A third purpose God has for sex is...

_____

_____

_____

God's purposes for sex in marriage are summed up by three key words:

Procreation: Sex is intended for the procreation of children. God's command to "be fruitful and multiply" has not changed or been revoked.

Pleasure: Sex is intended for the pleasure and enjoyment of the man and woman. Contrary to the interpretations of the medieval church, God is the author of sexual pleasure, not the censor.

Protection: Sex is intended to protect a husband and wife from temptation. Failure to sexually satisfy each other in marriage may lead to a spouse looking outside the marriage for fulfillment.

6. Which of these purposes is a surprise or a new insight to you?

    _____

    _____

    _____

    _____

    How does this new understanding affect your view of sex?

    _____

    _____

    _____

    _____

7. Do you have difficulty accepting any of these purposes for sex? If so, why?

    _____

    _____

    _____

    _____

Understanding Our Differences

Researchers continue to observe consistent differences in the attitudes,

needs and responses men and women bring into a sexual relationship, thus confirming God's purpose in creating us "male" and
"female." We are different and distinct. Understanding these differences in the sexual area is foundational to developing a healthy and
mutually satisfying sex life.

8.   Read through the following chart and circle anything that you
     did not realize before or anything that stands out to you.
     Note: These are in general commonly observed differences
     not concrete facts. Don't use this chart to determine how you
     ought to be. Use it to better help your fiancé(e) to understand
     you and for you to understand your fiancé(e).

Commonly Observed Differences in Sexuality		
	Men	**Women**
Attitude	Physical Compartmentalized	Relational Wholistic
Stimulation	Body-centered Sight Smell Actions	Person-centered Touch Attitudes Words
Needs	Respect To be physically needed Physical expression	Respect To be emotionally needed Relational intimacy
Sexual Response	Acyclical Quick excitement Difficult to distract	Cyclical Slow excitement Easily distracted
Orgasm	Shorter, more intense More physically oriented	Longer, more in-depth More emotionally oriented

9. What potential sexual problems can be anticipated in a marriage because men are generally more oriented toward the physical act of sex while women are more relationally oriented? How can you address these differences?

    _____

    _____

    _____

    _____

10. Why is it important for men to realize that women usually require more time to become sexually aroused?

    _____

    _____

    _____

    _____

11. Why is it important for women to realize the deep desire within men to be physically needed?

    _____

    _____

    _____

    _____

A Most Incredible Gift

In the context of a satisfying marriage relationship sex is the most personal and private act a husband and wife can share, a celebration of their unity and oneness. Sex in marriage is the physical expression of what is true of a couple on the emotional, mental and spiritual level. It is a wonderful gift God has given you! Don't be afraid to talk about it and don't worry about what other couples are doing. Enjoy each other!

navigating by true north

TRUTHS TO CHART YOUR COURSE

- Because sex is God's idea, growing in our relationship with Him is the most important thing we can do to develop our sex life.
- Sex is not an act, but a process of intimate communication.
- God's purposes for sex are: procreation, pleasure, and protection.
- Understanding and discussing expectations will alleviate fears, disarm potential bombshells, and head potential conflicts off at the pass.
- Understanding your differences, as male and female, is foundational to developing a healthy, mutually satisfying sex life.
- Sex is the physical *expression* of what is true of a couple on the emotional, mental, physical, and spiritual level.

Couple's Project

get real

1. Spend a few minutes sharing and discussing your answers to the questions in "Get the Picture" and "Get the Truth." Be sure to ask your fiancé(e) to explain his or her answers.

2. From your observations of the chart on page 218 titled "Commonly Observed Differences in Sexuality," complete the following phrase individually and then share your answers with each other:

   What I need you to understand about me from this chart is that because I am a man/woman…

   _____

   _____

   _____

   _____

3. Individually, write down three things you are eagerly anticipating in your sexual relationship and three things you are fearfully anxious about.

Anticipation	Anxiety

a. Share your answers with each other.

b. Ask your fiancé(e) what you can do now, or later, to alle-
    viate or address the most pressing anxiety issue.

4. Which one of the following weather phenomenon best express-
    es what you *anticipate* your honeymoon night will be like?

    ❑ A tornado: Focused, fast moving, intense, wild and unpre-
      dictable
    ❑ A hurricane: Powerful, methodical, slow moving, calm
      surrounded by incredible turbulence
    ❑ A blizzard: Wind chill at 20 degrees below zero, every-
      thing comes to a standstill, whipping sleet followed by
      pristine wispy blankets of sparkling snow
    ❑ A thunderstorm: A little of everything—lightning, thun-
      der, wind, rain, hail
    ❑ Heat lightning: Electrical fireworks off in the distance,
      but nothing really happens where you are
    ❑ Soaking rain: A cold, depressing shower that dampens
      your enthusiasm

    a. Explain your answer to your fiancé(e).
    b. Discuss any differing expectations you may have.

5. What is your view regarding birth control?

    _____

    _____

    _____

    _____

6. What are the most important insights you have gained about
    God's design for sexual intimacy from this session?

    _____

    _____

    _____

    _____

get to the heart of your marriage—prayer

MAKING PRAYER A PRIORITY COMMITMENT

Probably no other spiritual discipline has encouraged intimacy between a man and woman in marriage more than prayer. Daily prayer together as a couple will result in innumerable benefits to you as a couple. One of those benefits is emotional closeness that enables a couple to connect to God and one another on a daily basis. When we pray with and for one another it demands that we have forgiven one another. Prayer together enhances not only spiritual and emotional oneness, but also physical oneness.

Would you be willing to commit to your fiancé(e) that you will pray together daily? If so, write out a commitment to God that both of you will sign.

OUR PRAYER COMMITMENT

Signed_____ Date _____

Signed_____ Date _____

 # GET DEEPER

For more information on sexual intimacy, we suggest reading *Intended for Pleasure* by Ed Wheat, M.D. and Gaye Wheat; Fleming H. Revell, 1981.

QUESTIONS FOR THOSE WHO WERE PREVIOUSLY MARRIED

Answer the following questions individually, then share your answers with your fiancé(e).

1. How are you going to handle comparison to your previous spouse in this area?

   _____

   _____

   _____

   _____

2. List any wounds—emotional, physical, spiritual or mental— that you need to work through personally and with your fiancé(e).

   _____

   _____

   _____

   _____

3. Ask your fiancé(e) what his or her questions or fears are concerning this area of your future marriage in light of your and/or his or her previous marriage. Record your answers and talk about how you can work through these issues.

   _____

   _____

   _____

   _____

BONUS

tHe Past:
HOW MUCH DO
I sHaRe?

We live in a promiscuous age in which people promote safe, pro-tected sex yet ignore the terrible damage that sex outside of God's provision of marriage does to the human heart. An entire generation is marrying and remarrying with deep wounds and scars caused by its past choices. As couples contemplate marriage, they may look back with regret and guilt concerning choices they made in the past. Invariably they wonder, "Just how much of the past do I need to share with my fiancé(e)?"

This is not an easy question to answer, for several reasons:

- Sharing your past mistakes and sins may lead to shame-filled, painful moments between you as a couple.
- It may mean confessing a previously told lie to your fiancé(e).
- It may mean reliving incidents you'd rather not remember.
- It may result in a broken engagement.

You may be tempted to avoid sharing anything from your past; after all, as a Christian your sins are forgiven at the Cross, and the Bible says there is "no condemnation to those who are in Christ Jesus" (Romans 8:1).

While these things are true spiritually in our relationship with God, there are consequences of past sins that need to be honestly dealt with as a couple moves toward marriage. While you do not need to share every detail (as will be explained later), you cannot avoid the fact that your life has been shaped by your choices. If you and your fiancé(e) desire to make a solid decision about marriage, you need to be honest with each other and deal with your pasts. It is better to speak the truth prior to your marriage than to live with the fear, deceit and shame that comes from hiding the truth from your mate.

There is one other benefit to sharing your past. True healing can occur when you confess your sins to one another. God can use marriage to heal individuals from past hurts that have haunted them for years. This is especially true when dealing with sexual immorality in the past. Many men and women have found forgiveness, grace and liberty by confessing these scarring circumstances to their would-be spouses.

These are not easy issues to discuss. And there are no cookie-cutter solutions to what you may be struggling with. In an effort to guide those who are struggling with knowing what to do and how to go about it, here are a few principles and perspectives:

FOR THE PERSON WHO IS BURDENED WITH SOMETHING THAT SHOULD BE SHARED

1. Write out a list of all that you are feeling a need to share with your fiancé(e). This might include events, choices or hurts you've experienced. While you don't need to go into great detail, be sure to mention anything that you know will affect your relationship today (specific problems such as physical/emotional abuse, sexually transmitted diseases, etc.).

2. Once you've completed your list, make sure you have experienced God's forgiveness and cleansing for everything you've written. If you have not, spend some time in prayer, repenting and confessing your sin. You will experience God's forgiveness on the basis of 1 John 1:9 that tells us, "If we confess our sins, He is faithful and righteous to forgive us our sins and to cleanse us from all unrighteousness."

3. Determine which items on your list you should discuss with your fiancé(e), and why. *If you have doubts about any items, make sure you seek wise and godly counsel before talking with your fiancé(e).* Another person's compassionate listening ear and prayerful concern can guide you before and after you marry.

4. Set a time and place to share with your fiancé(e). Choose a private setting where you are both free to express your emotions.

5. Before you meet, pray that your fiancé(e) will have the strength and grace to respond in a loving manner. But don't go into the meeting expecting immediate forgiveness; your fiancé(e) may need time to work through emotions and think about what he or she has heard from you.

6. As you talk with your fiancé(e), explain why you think it's important to share these choices from your past, but *avoid sharing more than is necessary*. Be careful about sharing too many explicit details, as this can become a problem later in your marriage. By going into too much detail, you may give the one you love too much of the picture. Avoid morbid curiosity.

7. Give your fiancé(e) the time he or she needs to process this new information. This process may include hurt, anger or withdrawal.

8. If it becomes apparent that either of you cannot get beyond the hurt from what has been shared, seek wise counsel together or individually. If forgiveness and reconciliation cannot occur at this point, then we suggest delaying the wedding or breaking the engagement. If God is calling you to marriage, then His perfect love will be manifested in your hearts for one another. And His Word tells us, "perfect love casts out fear" (1 John 4:18).

FOR THE ONE HEARING THE CONFESSION

If you find yourself in the situation where your fiancé(e) is confessing something from the past to you, be encouraged by three things:

1. Listen carefully to what your fiancé(e) is sharing. Ask yourself, *Why did he/she come to me with this?* Look beyond the past and its ugliness to the broken heart that is sharing.

2. Consider your own condition before God—a sinner saved by grace. There is another reason why sharing the past is so difficult: We are all flawed as humans. Because we don't love perfectly and we pridefully believe that we deserve perfection, we can be tempted to condemn another for a past failure, whereas God calls us to forgive one another. *Remember how much He has forgiven you!*

    For example: If you have maintained your virginity, you may find yourself engaged to someone who has not. Often the one who is a virgin finds it very difficult to forgive and move beyond the fiancé(e)'s failure. Interestingly, young men who have kept their virginity have a much more difficult time forgiving.

3.   While you may legitimately decide that, given this new information about your fiancé(e), marriage is not wise, don't let pride prevent you from responding with love and forgiveness when your fiancé(e) is willing to share the mistakes from the past.

A final note: After you marry, it will be very important that neither of you use the things you learn here as ammunition in an argument. Forgiveness is an essential part of marriage and when we forgive, we give up the right to punish.

a fiNaL PROject

Congratulations on completing *Preparing for Marriage*! You've worked hard to reach this point and we trust that God has used this process to draw you closer to Him and to each other. If He is leading you to marry, the principles you've learned here and the communication experienced will provide the foundation for a oneness marriage.

Now that you've finished the workbook, here are a few final suggestions:

1. Turn to "Special Project 2: A Decision-Making Guide." If you have not worked through the process of making your decision about marriage, do so now.

    If you *have* worked through it, take a moment to look over your answers. Do you still have the same convictions about your partner and about your potential marriage?

    _____

    _____

    _____

    _____

    _____

    _____

2. Are you ready to receive your partner as God's provision for you? If so, sign the following statement and date it:

I can wholeheartedly receive _____
as God's perfect provision for my marriage partner for a
lifetime.

_____

Date _____

---

3. Select a Scripture verse that you will build upon as a foundation for your future marriage and family. For example, one couple chose Proverbs 3:3 which says, "Do not let kindness and truth leave you; bind them around your neck, write them on the tablet of your heart." They took the words "kindness" and "truth" and had them inscribed in each of their wedding rings. These two words serve as reminders to them of the foundational pillars on which they want their home to be founded to last a lifetime.

4. Deuteronomy 24:5 says:

> "When a man takes a new wife, he shall not go out with the army, nor be charged with any duty; he shall be free at home one year and shall give happiness to his wife whom he has taken."

While you may not be in the military, you would be wise to take the advice of this passage and devote the first year of your marriage to developing your relationship. Make a habit of saying no to many of your activities and continually say yes to being with each other the first year. You will have a lifetime after the first year to focus on others. This time of commitment will build a solid base for your marriage.

5. Many of the principles found in this workbook are taken from the FamilyLife Marriage Conference and from studies in the HomeBuilders Couples Series®. If you have the opportunity to attend a conference or one of the home Bible studies in your city, take it! Call 1-800-333-1433 for more information or write FamilyLife, 3900 N. Rodney Parham, Little Rock, AR 72212.

Purity Covenant

From the world's viewpoint, maintaining sexual purity before marriage seems like cruel and unusual punishment. Many people consider it strange if a couple does not sleep together before they are married. "After all," they say, "shouldn't they find out whether they are sexually compatible?"

As Session Six explains more clearly, God's Word regarding sex cuts right across the grain of our culture. The culture portrays sexual intimacy between two unmarried people as something as casual and innocuous as holding hands, but nothing could be further from the truth.

Read the following verses and seek to understand God's perspective of sex. Remember: Sex is God's idea.

> You shall not commit adultery (Exodus 20:14).

> Now flee from youthful lusts, and pursue righteousness, faith, love and peace, with those who call on the Lord from a pure heart (2 Timothy 2:22).

> Just as He chose us in Him before the foundation of the world, that we should be holy and blameless before Him (Ephesians 1:4).

As obedient children, do not be conformed to the former lusts which were yours in your ignorance, but like the Holy One who called you, be holy yourselves also in all your behavior; because it is written, "YOU SHALL BE HOLY, FOR I AM HOLY" (1 Peter 1:14-16).

Now for this very reason also, applying all diligence, in your faith supply moral excellence, and in your moral excellence, knowledge; and in your knowledge, self-control, and in your self-control, perseverance, and in your perseverance, godliness; and in your godliness, brotherly kindness, and in your brotherly kindness, love (2 Peter 1:5-7).

For this you know with certainty, that no immoral or impure person or covetous man, who is an idolater, has an inheritance in the kingdom of Christ and God (Ephesians 5:5).

Let marriage be held in honor among all, and let the marriage bed be undefiled; for fornicators and adulterers God will judge (Hebrews 13:4).

Finally, brethren, whatever is true, whatever is honorable, whatever is right, whatever is pure, whatever is lovely, whatever is of good repute, if there is any excellence and if anything worthy of praise, let your mind dwell on these things (Philippians 4:8).

But I want you to be wise in what is good, and innocent in what is evil (Romans 16:19).

It is easy to know another person sexually, especially in our present culture. But a marriage relationship requires much, much more than physical intimacy. There first needs to be spiritual and emotional intimacy to build trust, commitment and communication. Marriage is a lifelong covenant to love and care and nourish.

God had our best in mind when He gave us strong directives about sexual purity before marriage. There are many benefits to staying pure before marriage. By waiting until marriage:

- ❑ You please God.
- ❑ You build trust and trust is necessary for intimacy.
- ❑ You develop the godly qualities of patience and self-control.
- ❑ You affirm that you care more for the other person than for yourself.
- ❑ You protect yourself from feelings of guilt and shame.
- ❑ You provide yourself with an example to give your children.
- ❑ You are protected from emotional, mental and physical trauma should you break off your relationship.
- ❑ You develop healthy communication habits and skills.
- ❑ You avoid the possibility of an unwanted pregnancy.
- ❑ You maintain a clear conscience before God and man.
- ❑ You increase the anticipation and enjoyment of your wedding night.
- ❑ You experience the blessing of obedience.
- ❑ You discover more about each other than just the physical.
- ❑ You maintain a witness to a lost world.
- ❑ You keep from bringing reproach on the name of Christ.

Make a check mark beside the five benefits that strike a chord in your heart. Share these benefits and why you chose them.

Moral Excellence

Sexual purity is especially difficult during the engagement period. You have declared your commitment and you naturally want to consummate the relationship. You may even feel married at points. Yet what better time to establish your relationship and build trust in one another by obeying God than on this key point.

Sexual purity means much more than not having sexual intercourse before marriage. Many couples avoid intercourse but are still sexually intimate. Look again at the verses quoted previously. Scripture defines sexual purity as being morally excellent. And moral excellence means *being holy*. It means avoiding the appearance of evil. It means purity of thought as well as purity of deed. It means protecting one another's innocence from being stained by evil.

OUR CHALLENGE TO YOU IS TO DO MUCH MORE
THAN REMAIN ABSTINENT UNTIL YOUR MARRIAGE.
OUR CHALLENGE IS TO BE PURE.

1. Without writing anything that would embarrass you or your fiancé(e), write out what you two have agreed would be the limits and boundaries in the sexual area of your relationship:

_____

_____

_____

_____

2. What has been your practice/experience up to this point in your relationship?

_____

_____

_____

_____

3. How do you feel about your practice/experience up to this point?

_____

_____

_____

_____

4. Now write a one sentence definition for moral excellence as it relates to your physical relationship.
Moral excellence in our physical relationship means...

_____

_____

_____

_____

5. Based on your definition, check the boxes that give you specific boundaries that you believe God wants you to hold to in your physical relationship.

    ❏ We will not kiss until the wedding ceremony.
    ❏ We will not be alone after 10 P.M.
    ❏ We will not lie next to each other in any setting.
    ❏ We will not fondle or pet each other.
    ❏ We will not give each other massages.
    ❏ We will not do anything that we would be embarrassed to tell Jesus we did.
    ❏ We will not touch each other anywhere that clothing would normally cover.
    ❏ Other _____

As you understand God's desire for your moral purity, pray and ask God to show you if there is anything that you need to apologize to your fiancé(e) for and seek forgiveness in this area. If there is, take the time to address it now in prayer with God and with your fiancé(e).

Remember, 1 John 1:9 says that "if we confess our sins"—agree with God concerning our sin—"He is faithful and righteous to forgive us our sins and to cleanse us from all unrighteousness." You can start right now with a clean slate.

After discussing this with your fiancé(e), it may be appropriate for you both to confess this to your mentor couple, ask them to pray for you, help you set limits and hold you accountable to them.

Purity Covenant

1. Take the Purity Covenant and place it before you. Read through the sections one at a time.
2. After you have read through all three passages and commitments, sign and date the Covenant.
3. If they are not with you, have your mentor couple/pastor/counselor sign the Purity Covenant at your next meeting. They will ask you if you are honoring your covenant before signing.

PURITY COVENANT

BIBLICAL STANDARD

1 Thessalonians 4:3-8: "For this is the will of God, your sanctification; that is, that you abstain from sexual immorality; that each of you know how to possess his own vessel in sanctification and honor, not in lustful passion, like the Gentiles who do not know God; and that no man transgress and defraud his brother in the matter because the Lord is the avenger in all these things, just as we also told you before and solemnly warned you. For God has not called us for the purpose of impurity, but in sanctification. Consequently, he who rejects this is not rejecting man but the God who gives His Holy Spirit to you."

IN OBEDIENCE TO GOD'S COMMAND, I PROMISE
TO PROTECT YOUR SEXUAL PURITY FROM
THIS DAY UNTIL OUR HONEYMOON.

BIBLICAL STANDARD

1 Corinthians 6:18-20: "Flee immorality. Every other sin that a man commits is outside the body, but the immoral man sins against his own body. Or do you not know that your body is a temple of the Holy Spirit who is in you, whom you have from God, and that you are not your own? For you have been bought with a price: therefore glorify God in your body."

BECAUSE I RESPECT AND HONOR YOU, I COMMIT
TO BUILDING UP THE INNER PERSON OF YOUR
HEART RATHER THAN VIOLATING YOU.

BIBLICAL STANDARD

Acts 24:16: "In view of this, I also do my best to maintain always a blameless conscience both before God and before men."

I PLEDGE TO SHOW MY LOVE FOR YOU IN WAYS
THAT ALLOW BOTH OF US TO MAINTAIN A CLEAR
CONSCIENCE BEFORE GOD AND EACH OTHER.

This is my promise of purity.

Signed _____   Signed _____

Date _____   Date _____

Witnessed/affirmed by _____

Date _____

the four spiritual Laws*

Just as there are physical laws that govern the physical universe, so are there spiritual laws that govern your relationship with God.

LAW ONE: GOD LOVES YOU AND OFFERS A WONDERFUL PLAN FOR YOUR LIFE.

God's Love

"For God so loved the world, that He gave His only begotten Son, that whoever believes in Him should not perish, but have eternal life" (John 3:16).

God's Plan

(Christ speaking) "I came that they might have life, and might have it abundantly" (that it might be full and meaningful) (John 10:10).

Why is it that most people are not experiencing the abundant life? Because...

LAW TWO: MAN IS SINFUL AND SEPARATED FROM GOD. THEREFORE, HE CANNOT KNOW AND EXPERIENCE GOD'S LOVE AND PLAN FOR HIS LIFE.

Man Is Sinful

"For all have sinned and fall short of the glory of God" (Romans 3:23).

Man was created to have fellowship with God; but, because of his stubborn self-will, chose to go his own independent way, and fellowship with God was broken. This self-will, characterized by an attitude of active rebellion or passive indifference, is evidence of what the Bible calls sin.

Man Is Separated

"For the wages of sin is death" (spiritual separation from God) (Romans 6:23).

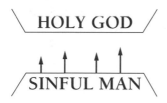

This diagram illustrates that God is holy and man is sinful. A great gulf separates the two. The arrows illustrate that man is continually trying to reach God and the abundant life through his own efforts, such as a good life, philosophy, or religion.

The third law explains the only way to bridge this gulf...

LAW THREE: JESUS CHRIST IS GOD'S ONLY PROVISION FOR MAN'S SIN. THROUGH HIM YOU CAN KNOW AND EXPERIENCE GOD'S LOVE AND PLAN FOR YOUR LIFE.

He Died in Our Place

"But God demonstrates His own love toward us, in that while we were yet sinners, Christ died for us" (Romans 5:8).

He Rose from the Dead

"Christ died for our sins . . . He was buried . . . He was raised on the third day according to the Scriptures . . . He appeared to [Peter], then to the twelve. After that He appeared to more than five hundred . . ." (1 Corinthians 15:3-6).

He Is the Only Way to God

"Jesus said to him, 'I am the way, and the truth, and the life; no one comes to the Father, but through Me'" (John 14:6).

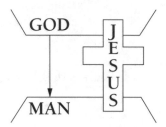

This diagram illustrates that God has bridged the gulf that separates us from Him by sending His Son, Jesus Christ, to die on the cross in our place to pay the penalty for our sins. It is not enough just to know these three laws...

> **LAW FOUR: WE MUST INDIVIDUALLY RECEIVE JESUS CHRIST AS SAVIOR AND LORD; THEN WE CAN KNOW AND EXPERIENCE GOD'S LOVE AND PLAN FOR OUR LIVES.**

We Must Receive Christ

"But as many as received Him, to them He gave the right to become children of God, even to those who believe in His name" (John 1:12).

We Receive Christ Through Faith

"For by grace you have been saved through faith; and that not of yourselves, it is the gift of God; not as a result of works, that no one should boast" (Ephesians 2:8,9).

When We Receive Christ, We Experience a New Birth

(Read John 3:1-8).

We Receive Christ by Personal Invitation

(Christ is speaking) "Behold, I stand at the door and knock; if any one hears My voice and opens the door, I will come in to him" (Revelation 3:20).

Receiving Christ involves turning to God from self (repentance) and trusting Christ to come into our lives to forgive our sins and to make us the kind of people He wants us to be. Just to agree intellectually that Jesus Christ is the Son of God and that He died on the cross for our sins is not enough. Nor is it enough to have an emotional experience. We receive Jesus Christ by faith, as an act of the will.

These two circles represent two kinds of lives:

SELF-DIRECTED LIFE
S - Self is on the throne
† - Christ is outside of the life
• - Interests are directed by self, often resulting in discord and frustration

CHRIST-DIRECTED LIFE
† - Christ is in the life and on the throne
S - Self is yielding to Christ
• - Interests are directed by Christ, resulting in harmony with God's plan

Which circle best represents your life?
Which circle would you like to have represent your life?

The following explains how you can receive Christ:

You Can Receive Christ Right Now by Faith Through Prayer

(Prayer is talking with God).

God knows your heart and is not so concerned with your words as He is with the attitude of your heart. The following is a suggested prayer:

> LORD JESUS, I NEED YOU. THANK YOU FOR DYING ON THE CROSS FOR MY SINS. I OPEN THE DOOR OF MY LIFE AND RECEIVE YOU AS MY SAVIOR AND LORD. THANK YOU FOR FORGIVING MY SINS AND GIVING ME ETERNAL LIFE. MAKE ME THE KIND OF PERSON YOU WANT ME TO BE.

Does this prayer express the desire of your heart?

If it does, pray this prayer right now, and Christ will come into your life, as He promised.

*Written by Bill Bright. Copyright © Campus Crusade for Christ, Inc., 1965. All rights reserved.

Have you made the Wonderful Discovery of the Spirit-filled Life?

Every day can be an exciting adventure for the Christian who knows the reality of being filled with the Holy Spirit and who lives constantly, moment by moment, under His gracious control.

The Bible tells us that there are three kinds of people:

1. **Natural Man** (one who has not received Christ)
"But a natural man does not accept the things of the Spirit of God; for they are foolishness to him, and he cannot understand them, because they are spiritually appraised" (1 Corinthians 2:14).

SELF-DIRECTED LIFE
S - Self is on the throne
† - Christ is outside of the life
• - Interests are directed by self, often resulting in discord and frustration

2. **Spiritual Man** (one who is controlled and empowered by the Holy Spirit) "But he who is spiritual appraises all things..." (1 Corinthians 2:15).

CHRIST-DIRECTED LIFE
† - Christ is on the throne of the life
S - Ego or self is dethroned
• - Interests are under control of infinite God, resulting in harmony with God's plan

245

3. **Carnal Man** (one who has received Christ, but who lives in defeat because he trusts in his own efforts to live the Christian life).

SELF-DIRECTED LIFE
S - Ego or finite self is on the throne
† - Christ is dethroned
• - Interests controlled by self, often resulting in discord and frustration

"And I, brethren, could not speak to you as to spiritual men, but as to carnal men, as to babes in Christ. I gave you milk to drink, not solid food; for you were not yet able to receive it. Indeed, even now you are not yet able, for you are still carnal. For since there is jealousy and strife among you, are you not fleshly, and are you not walking like mere men?" (1 Corinthians 3:1-3).

A. God Has Provided for Us an Abundant and Fruitful Christian Life.

Jesus said, "I came that they might have life, and might have it abundantly" (John 10:10).

"I am the vine, you are the branches; he who abides in Me, and I in him, he bears much fruit; for apart from Me you can do nothing" (John 15:5).

"But the fruit of the Spirit is love, joy, peace, patience, kindness, goodness, faithfulness, gentleness, self-control; against such things there is no law" (Galatians 5:22,23).

"But you shall receive power when the Holy Spirit has come upon you; and you shall be My witnesses both in Jerusalem, and in all Judea and Samaria, and even to the remotest part of the earth" (Acts 1:8).

the spiritual man

Some personal traits that result from trusting God:

Christ-centered
Empowered by the Holy Spirit
Introduces others to Christ
Effective prayer life
Understands God's Word
Trusts God
Obeys God

Love
Joy
Peace
Patience
Kindness
Goodness
Faithfulness

The degree to which these traits are manifested in the life depends upon the extent to which the Christian trusts the Lord with every detail of his, life, and upon his maturity in Christ. One who is only beginning to understand the ministry of the Holy Spirit should not be discouraged if he is not as fruitful as more mature Christians who have known and experienced this truth for a longer period.

Why is it that most Christians are not experiencing the abundant life?

B. Carnal Christians Cannot Experience the Abundant and Fruitful Christian Life

The carnal man trusts in his own efforts to live the Christian life:

1. He is either uninformed about, or has forgotten, God's love, forgiveness and power (Romans 5:8-10; Hebrews 10:1-25; 1 John 1; 2:1-3; 2 Peter 1:9; Acts 1:8).
2. He has an up-and-down spiritual experience.
3. He cannot understand himself—he wants to do what is right, but cannot.
4. He fails to draw upon the power of the Holy Spirit to live the Christian life (1 Corinthians 3:1-3; Romans 7:15-24; 8:7; Galatians 5:16-18).

tHe caRNaL maN

Some or all of the following traits may characterize the Christian who does not fully trust God:

Ignorance of his spiritual heritage
Unbelief
Disobedience
Loss of love for God and for others
Poor prayer life
No desire for Bible study

Legalistic attitude
Discouragement
Impure thoughts
Jealousy
Guilt
Critical Spirit
Worry
Frustration
Aimlessness

(The individual who professes to be a Christian but who continues to practice sin should realize that he may not be a Christian at all, according to 1 John 2:3; 3:6,9; Ephesians 5:5).

The third truth gives us the only solution to this problem…

C. Jesus Promised the Abundant and Fruitful Life as the Result of Being Filled (Controlled and Empowered) by the Holy Spirit

The Spirit-filled life is the Christ-controlled life by which Christ lives His life in and through us in the power of the Holy Spirit (John 15).

1. One becomes a Christian through the ministry of the Holy Spirit, according to John 3:1-8. From the moment of spiritual birth, the Christian is indwelt by the Holy Spirit at all times (John 1:12; Colossians 2:9,10; John 14:16,17). Though all Christians are indwelt by the Holy Spirit, not all Christians are filled (controlled and empowered) by the Holy Spirit.

2. The Holy Spirit is the source of the overflowing life (John 7:37-39).

3. The Holy Spirit came to glorify Christ (John 16:1-5). When one is filled with the Holy Spirit, he is a true disciple of Christ.

4. In His last command before His Ascension, Christ promised the power of the Holy Spirit to enable us to be witnesses for Him (Acts 1:1-9).

How, then, can one be filled with the Holy Spirit?

D. We Are Filled (Controlled and Empowered) by the Holy Spirit by Faith; Then We Can Experience the Abundant and Fruitful Life That Christ Promised to Each Christian.

You can appropriate the filling of the Holy Spirit right now if you:

1. Sincerely desire to be controlled and empowered by the Holy Spirit (Matthew 5:6; John 7:37-39).

2. Confess your sins.
    By faith thank God that He has forgiven all of your sins—past, present and future—because Christ died for you (Colossians 2:13-15; 1 John 1; 2:1-3; Hebrews 10:1-17).

3. By faith claim the fullness of the Holy Spirit, according to:
    a. HIS COMMAND—Be filled with the Spirit. "And do not get drunk with wine, for that is dissipation, but be filled with the Spirit" (Ephesians 5:18).
    b. HIS PROMISE—He will always answer when we pray according to His will. "And this is the confidence which we have before Him, that, if we ask anything according to His will, He hears us. And if we know that He hears us in whatever we ask, we know that we have the requests which we have asked from Him" (1 John 5:14,15).

Faith can be expressed through prayer...

How to Pray in Faith to Be Filled with the Holy Spirit

We are filled with the Holy Spirit by faith alone. However, true prayer is one way of expressing your faith. The following is a suggested prayer:

> Dear Father, I need You. I acknowledge that I have been in control of my life; and that, as a result, I have sinned against You. I thank You that You have forgiven my sins through Christ's death on the cross for me. I now invite Christ to again take control of the throne of my life. Fill me with the Holy Spirit as You commanded me to be filled, and as You promised in your Word that You would do if I asked in faith. I pray this in the name of Jesus. As an expression of my faith, I now thank You for taking control of my life and for filling me with the Holy Spirit.

Does this prayer express the desire of your heart? If so, bow in prayer and trust God to fill you with the Holy Spirit right now.

How to Know That You Are Filled (Controlled and Empowered) by the Holy Spirit

Did you ask God to fill you with the Holy Spirit? Do you know that you are now filled with the Holy Spirit? On what authority? (On the trustworthiness of God Himself and His Word: Hebrews 11:6; Romans 14:22,23.)

Do not depend upon feelings. The promise of God's Word, not our feelings, is our authority. The Christian lives by faith (trust) in the trustworthiness of God Himself and His Word. This train diagram illustrates the relationship between fact (God and His Word), faith (our trust in God and His Word), and feeling (the result of our faith and obedience) (John 14:21).

The train will run with or without the caboose. However, it would be futile to attempt to pull the train by the caboose. In the same way, we, as Christians, do not depend upon feelings or emotions, but we place our faith (trust) in the trustworthiness of God and the promises of His Word.

How to Walk in the Spirit

Faith (trust in God and His promises) is the only means by which a Christian can live the Spirit-controlled life. As you continue to trust Christ moment by moment:

1. Your life will demonstrate more and more of the fruit of the Spirit (Galatians 5:22,23); and will be more and more conformed to the image of Christ (Romans 12:2; 2 Corinthians 3:18).
2. Your prayer life and study of God's Word will become more meaningful.
3. You will experience His power in witnessing (Acts 1:8).

4. You will be prepared for spiritual conflict against the world (1 John 2:15-17); against the flesh (Galatians 5:16,17); and against Satan (1 Peter 5:7-9; Ephesians 6:10-13).

5. You will experience His power to resist temptation and sin (1 Corinthians 10:13; Philippians 4:13; Ephesians 1:19-23; 6:10; 2 Timothy 1:7; Romans 6;1-16).

Spiritual Breathing

By faith you can continue to experience God's love and forgiveness.

If you become aware of an area of your life (an attitude or an action) that is displeasing to the Lord, even though you are walking with Him and sincerely desiring to serve Him, simply thank God that He has forgiven your sins—past, present and future—on the basis of Christ's death on the cross. Claim His love and forgiveness by faith and continue to have fellowship with Him.

If you retake the throne of your life through sin—a definite act of disobedience—breathe spiritually.

Spiritual Breathing (exhaling the impure and inhaling the pure) is an exercise in faith that enables you to continue to experience God's love and forgiveness.

1. Exhale—confess your sin—agree with God concerning your sin and thank Him for His forgiveness of it, according to 1 John 1:9 and Hebrews 10:1-25. Confession involves repentance—a change in attitude and action.

2. Inhale—surrender the control of your life to Christ, and appropriate (receive) the fullness of the Holy Spirit by faith. Trust that He now controls and empowers you, according to the command of Ephesians 5:18, and the promise of 1 John 5:14,15.

about the authors

David Boehi is the editor of Real FamilyLife magazine and of the HomeBuilders Couple's Series®.

Jeff Schulte and **Lloyd Shadrach** are former FamilyLife staff members who are now pastors in Nashville, Tennessee.

Brent Nelson is also a former FamilyLife staff member who presently works as a salesman in Birmingham, Alabama.

about the general editor

Dennis Rainey is Executive Director of FamilyLife, host of "FamilyLife Today" radio show and the author of several best-selling books, including *Moments Together for Couples* (Regal Books, 1995).

Bless Your Home.

Marriage-building resources from Regal Books.

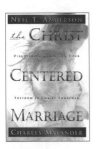

The Christ-Centered Marriage

Neil T. Anderson and Charles Mylander

This engaging book will show you and your spouse how to work together to securely set your marriage on a Christ-centered foundation and experience renewed intimacy, joy and fulfillment.

Paperback
ISBN 08307.18494

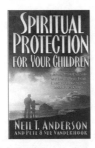

Spiritual Protection for Your Children

Neil T. Anderson and Pete & Sue Vander Hook

This is the incredible true story of a family that found themselves at the center of a satanic assault. This book will equip you to resist the enemy and protect your children by claiming your family's identity in Christ.

Paperback
ISBN 08307.18680

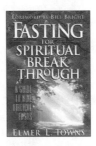

Fasting for Spiritual Breakthrough

Elmer Towns

This book explores the biblical foundations for fasting and introduces you to nine biblical fasts—each designed for a specific physical and spiritual outcome.

Paperback
ISBN 08307.18397

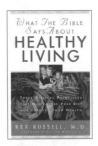

What the Bible Says About Healthy Living

Rex Russell, M.D.

The definitive diet plan taken straight from God's Word! These biblical principles for healthy eating and living will help you improve your physical—and spiritual—health.

Paperback
ISBN 08307.18583

Moments Together for Couples

Dennis and Barbara Rainey

This easy-to-use, best-selling 365-day devotional will give you and your spouse a chance to pause, relax and draw upon the strength of the Lord every day.

Hardcover
ISBN 08307.17544

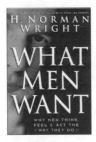

What Men Want

H. Norman Wright

Every man has questions. Here's a book with answers! For men, it's a clear look at God's plan for true manhood. For women, it's a revealing look at why men think and act the way they do.

Hardcover
ISBN 08307.15932

Starting Out Together Devotional

H. Norman Wright

A great beginning for dating or engaged couples, this dynamic 60-day devotional will help them to start their days and lives together focused on God.

Hardcover
ISBN 08307.18761

The Secrets of a Lasting Marriage

H. Norman Wright

Love can last for a lifetime. Here is a clear, practical plan to help couples reignite a love that is fading, or reinforce a love that is still going strong.

Hardcover
ISBN
08307.17498

Ask for these resources at your local Christian bookstore.

Regal
A Division of Gospel Light

Tools for a Family Reformation.

FAMILYLIFE CONFERENCES

FamilyLife Conferences are bringing meaningful, positive change to thousands of couples and families every year. The conferences, offered throughout the country, are based on solid biblical principles and are designed to provide couples and parents–in just one weekend–with the practical skills to build and enhance their marriages and families.

A Weekend to Remember.

The FamilyLife Marriage Conference gives you the opportunity to slow down and focus on your spouse and your relationship. You will spend an insightful weekend together, doing fun couples' projects and hearing from dynamic speakers on real-life solutions for building and enhancing oneness in your marriage.

Take a Weekend to Raise Your Children for a Lifetime!

The FamilyLife Parenting Conference will equip you with the principles and tools you need to be more effective parents for a lifetime. Whether you're just getting started or in the turbulent years of adolescence, you'll learn biblical blueprints for raising your children.

☞ **To register or recieve a free brochure and schedule for these conferences, call FamilyLife at 1-800-FL-TODAY.**

FAMILYLIFE TODAY RADIO PROGRAM

Tune In to Good News for Families.

Over 1,000,000 listeners across the nation are tuning in weekly to "FamilyLife Today," recently given the **1995 National Religious Broadcasters Radio Program Producer of the Year Award**. FamilyLife executive director Dennis Rainey and cohost Bob Lepine provide a fast-paced halfhour of interviews and address practical biblical issues your family faces. So tune in this week and take advantage of this unique opportunity to be encouraged in your marriage and family.

☞ **Call 1-800-FL-TODAY for the times and stations near you.**

REAL FAMILYLIFE MAGAZINE

A New Resource for Building Families.

Our brand-new magazine, *Real FamilyLife*, is designed to communicate practical, biblical truth on marriage and family. Each monthly issue features articles, columns, and projects by Dennis and Barbara Rainey and others who will help you build a godly family.

☞ **To receive more information about FamilyLife resources, call 1-800-FL-TODAY.**

For your marriage...   for your children...

for yourself...

for a lifetime.

FAMILYLIFE
Bringing Timeless Principles Home

P.O. Box 23840 • Little Rock, AR 72221-3840
(501) 223-8663 • 1-800-999-8663

A MINISTRY OF CAMPUS CRUSADE FOR CHRIST